CREDIT AND DEBT
The consumer interest

NATIONAL CONSUMER COUNCIL

LONDON: HMSO

(1990)

© Crown copyright 1990
First published 1990
ISBN 0 11 701215 7   18059953

Other National Consumer Council books published by HMSO:

Ordinary Justice
Legal services and the courts in England and Wales
ISBN 0 11 701369 2
1989 £11.95

In the Absence of Competition
A consumer view of public utilities regulation
ISBN 0 11 701211 4
1989 £9.95

Consumers and the Common Agricultural Policy
ISBN 0 11 701370 6
1988 £11.95

What's Wrong With Walking?
A consumer review of the pedestrian environment
ISBN 0 11 701271 8
1987 £4.95

Air Transport and the Consumer
A report on air transport regulation in Europe
ISBN 0 11 701268 8
1986 £7.95

British Library Cataloguing in Publication Data.

A CIP catalogue record for this book is available from the British Library.

Contents

4. The decision to lend: credit-granting and risk assessment

5. The National Consumer Council's recommendations

Foreword

People have always needed or wanted things they cannot immediately afford. And there have always been people on hand with the money to lend to them - at a cost.

This report looks back over the last ten years of consumers' experience with credit and debt, and looks forward to what may be happening in the next.

The 1980s were a time of rapid change. Consumers enormously increased their use of credit. New types of lending grew quickly, older ones declined in importance. Most people have been able to make good use of these new opportunities, but there has, too, been a worrying increase, for whatever reason, in the number of credit casualties.

And, as I write, the UK is about to embark on a new challenge - full participation in the expanded, highly competitive market of the European Community. What might be the outcome for consumer borrowing?

The change in economic conditions in the last year has reminded us that credit is a risk business. It is risky for lenders, of course, but it is risky for borrowers, too. Taking on credit means mortgaging your future, in a large or small way. And none of us can be certain about the future.

Today's rising casualty rate raises anxieties about the greater potential for damage in an expanded market. In particular, we want to prevent over-enthusiastic use of credit by undiscriminating and poorly informed consumers.

Many people are still forced by necessity to borrow - sometimes on contracts they do not understand, and at rates that, realistically, they may not be able to afford. On the other hand, more and more people are borrowing from choice - on credit cards, secured loans, and overdrafts. In either case, consumers can only make sensible choices if they understand how the odds are calculated. We all need to ensure that we are in control of the credit we take - and not the reverse.

Information and education are important keys. They are at the heart of a truly competitive and healthy credit market.

I hope that by working with the credit industry and government, we can ensure that today's borrowing will safeguard, and not jeopardise, our joint future.

Judith Wilcox,
Chairman, National Consumer Council

Acknowledgements

This book draws together, and develops, a number of National Consumer Council policy papers on the theme of consumer credit produced in the ten years since our last major review of the subject. Over this period, many past and present members of the Council have contributed to the development of our policy.

The final form of this book was overseen by the NCC's economic committee, chaired by John Hughes. The other members of the committee were Sheila Black OBE, Anthony Burton OBE, David Michaels, Ann Scully and Martin Wolf.

The text was written by Deborah Leonard with editorial help from Liz Dunbar and Maurice Healy of the National Consumer Council. Peter Grosvenor (formerly of the NCC) prepared a report on the UK social fund and an equivalent system in the Netherlands on which we have drawn. Stewart Dresner of *Privacy Laws and Business* supplied the material on the status of data protection law and the consumer credit information in other European countries (appendix IV.4). The text was typed by Eldorna Mapp and verified by Susan Foreman, Sarah Hack and Andrew Morris.

Thanks, too, to Richard Berthoud and Elaine Kempson of the Policy Studies Institute, to Simon Moulton at the Office of the Data Protection Registrar, and to other colleagues for commenting on drafts, and to Brian Lord and staff at CCN Systems Ltd for providing a hypothetical credit reference file (appendix IV.2).

About this review

When the National Consumer Council published its first comprehensive investigation of consumer credit ten years ago (*Consumers and Credit*, NCC, 1980), the level of personal borrowing - excluding mortgages and fuel bills - was around £11 billion. The equivalent figure today is well over £43 billion. The rise and rise of consumer credit over the ten years has been underpinned by an expansion in new sources of credit and new types of lender and by the liberalisation of financial markets. Running in parallel has been a shift in people's attitudes towards personal borrowing and spending. As a nation we have thrown away the piggy bank on the mantelpiece and now rely on future income to buy what we want today.

As we shall see in this review, this has not been a painless process. There have been, and there still are, serious consumer casualties on the road to financial sophistication.

The National Consumer Council has worked on many aspects of credit and default over the ten years since the publication of *Consumers and Credit*. In establishing and tracking our policies, we have become increasingly concerned that the findings and conclusions of that 1979/80 study are less applicable to the 1990s. It was made at a time of deepening economic recession and relatively limited credit availability and, in 1979/80, while we anticipated a growth in the financial market generally, we were less clear about its speed and extent.

New surveys have been published, notably by the Office of Fair Trading, which provide substantial new evidence on consumer attitudes and behaviour. Our 1979/80 study - commissioned by the government with the specific brief to examine personal credit and the effects of the 1974 Consumer Credit Act - did not discuss the implications of borrowing for house purchase. We are conscious, too, of the fiercer competition within the expanding financial services market and the potential effects of the completion of the single European market in 1992.

It was against this background of dramatic changes and shifting perspectives that we undertook this review of consumers' financial behaviour, needs and trends ten years on. It includes detailed discussion of home loans - a driving force in the expansion of consumer credit; the so-called 'proxy credit' of deferred payment of fuel and water bills; and local authority and welfare credit in the form of housing benefit and social fund loans.

HOW THE REVIEW IS ORGANISED

The book starts with a broad view of the issues important to a consumer review of credit and debt, and outlines the major areas for debate in the 1990s, as we see them.

Section 1 outlines the facts and figures on personal borrowing over the past ten years and section 2 discusses some of the underlying trends and influences that have shaped those facts.

In section 3 we discuss the consumer issues. We highlight groups of consumers particularly at risk of moving from manageable household budgeting to overcommitment and insolvency, and two specific credit products that we believe need close monitoring. Also in this section we discuss the information and the attitudes that affect consumers' decisions when they are shopping for credit.

In section 4 we focus on the strategies and techniques used by lenders for assessing creditworthiness and granting credit - an important dimension of the credit industry.

In section 5 we identify some concerns over the whole field of consumer credit and debt, and propose some action. Our recommendations are addressed to government, the lending institutions and credit reference agencies.

The detailed tables and figures that fill out the discussion all appear in the appendices. Some of the data have been difficult to compile. The official figures are often scattered or incomplete, and changes in the way they are reported, combined with rapid changes in the financial services market itself, mean that it is not always possible to give fully comparable information on trends. We try to explain the basis of each analysis in the tables and the text, and a note at the start of the appendices outlines some specific problems.

THE CONSUMER INTEREST

A byproduct of credit is debt, and unmanageable consumer debt is inevitably an important focus of this review.

The routes into personal debt are seldom simple, and are certainly seldom explained wholly by individual mismanagement, incompetence or misuse. Often more telling as indicators of financial problems are poverty, social deprivation and inequality, and these issues are threaded throughout our discussion.

In looking at debt from a consumer perspective, it is important neither to lump all commitments together into one huge overall figure nor to study each item of borrowing in isolation. We propose that a more realistic and rounded picture comes from looking at personal debt as a *network* of multiple commitment. We therefore examine different categories of borrower who take on different commitments at different times in their lives, and examine some of the consequences that arise from those networks.

SOME TERMS EXPLAINED

The words *debt* and *debtor* when applied to individual consumers have some pejorative connotations that make them unhelpful in a consumer policy review. Strictly speaking, nearly all of us are in debt. But we do not usually think of it this way when, for instance, we switch on the light and get electricity on credit.

So we more often use the word *commitment* to describe the act by which a consumer undertakes a financial agreement. 'Commitment' emphasises the specific obligation taken on by the borrower to repay. It also indicates a more general pledge, implied or explicit, to make full repayment. And, when used in an economic context, it can describe the amount and level of charges held against a person's assets.

Our report uses four informal categories of personal credit commitment, broadly covering the levels from 'manageable' to 'insolvent'. Below we illustrate the sorts of financial commitment that might fall into our four categories, although these are not mutually exclusive and are likely to overlap and merge with a change in people's circumstances.

(a) Manageable commitment:

when the borrower has one or more financial agreements and services them regularly and more or less on time. There are no - or only occasional - charges on revolving credit accounts. Income is adequate to meet all the household budget and credit commitments.

In effect, this is a system of precisely monitored *deferred payment*.

Manageable commitment is most likely to occur among older people and in families where there are no dependent children. It does not necessarily depend on an absolute minimum income level.

(b) Overcommitment:

when the borrower enters into one or more agreements and makes some repayments late. Commitments are in arrears, but by no more than two months; some repayments are made only with the final demand notice. The borrower nearly always incurs charges on revolving credit accounts and sometimes makes only minimum repayments. The borrower uses overdraft facilities regularly. Repayments become less precise in amount and regularity. Accounts are managed, but with difficulty.

Overcommitment is most common among younger adults, before they reach peak income, and in families with young or dependent children. Outgoings are often high in relation to income, and unpredictable, so that systematic budgeting is distorted. This level of commitment is probably the most common, and one that almost every household will experience at one time or another. It represents a margin within which it is probably 'safe' for a borrower to operate.

(c) Unmanageable commitment:

the borrower has one or more agreements. Some accounts are more than three months in arrears; other repayments are made late. This borrower often makes only minimum payments to cover interest charges and is in serious arrears for fuel, telephone or rent/mortgage. Fuel boards and local authorities serve final demands and summonses. Some items - like cars, or furniture on hire purchase - are repossessed. Budgets are controlled by crisis management.

This stage is sometimes an inevitable consequence of overcommitment. Sometimes an unexpected event like redundancy, bereavement or pregnancy throws out the household budgeting. Attempts to solve the problems earlier may have been inept or inadequate.

(d) Insolvency:

the borrower is systematically unable to meet commitments by the required date. All his/her remaining assets have been, or are about to be, repossessed.

Introduction: credit and debt in the 1990s

Money is consumers' most basic tool. Borrowing money is one crucial way for people to get the things they need (or want) at the time they need them. They satisfy current needs out of the expectation of future income. It is clear that this process creates both opportunity and risk: the opportunity to meet current need now and the risk that the expectation of future ability to repay may be wrong.

So it is not surprising that credit and debt have been an important preoccupation for the National Consumer Council since its earliest days. From 1978 to 1980 we carried out a major study, at the government's request, into consumers' use of credit. In our final report, *Consumers and Credit*, we concluded:

> "The general message of our work has been reassuring. We found no evidence of widespread serious credit problems, and a wide choice of credit generally available to people. People generally manage to get the sort of credit they want, and it is rare for them to be dissatisfied with it once they have got it."

And we said:

> "In general, as far as lenders and credit operators are concerned, we see more advantage in cooperation and persuasion than in rigid regulatory coercion; for most borrowers, educated self-help rather than cossetting."

In 1983 we followed up that report with *Consumers and Debt* (which we published jointly with the Welsh Consumer Council). Its message was that the traditional view of debtors as feckless incompetents was wrong. Debtors, research showed,

> "are very largely people who have suffered an unexpected drop in income - for such reasons as redundancy, short-time working, illness, a death in the family, or marriage break-up. In other words, income has gone down since they took on commitments which they are now unable to meet."

We proposed changes to the way the law treats debtors to provide a system better matched to solving the problems of the people who *cannot pay* rather than punishing people who *will not pay*.

In 1987, we reviewed the problems arising from the growing trend of people taking out loans, as well as first mortgages, secured on their homes. Our report, *Security Risks*, showed that while the vast majority of people who took out this sort of loan managed them perfectly well, some found themselves in serious difficulties. They were sold loans at very high interest rates without understanding that they were putting their homes at risk. We recommended that advertisements for such loans should specifically warn about this. The government has since introduced regulations to ensure that this happens.

The purpose of this review is to look back over the last ten years, to see how things have changed, and to look forward to what the problems and opportunities may be in the next ten years. Of course, an important factor in this will be our growing closeness to Europe. A wider market in credit will mean that some of the assumptions we have made about the regulation of credit in this country will face competition from different ideas and different traditions in other European countries.

What, then, has happened in the last ten years?

There is a lot more credit about. Both consumer credit indebtedness and mortgage borrowing have more than doubled in real terms since 1980. Consumers owe about twice as much on average per head as they did ten years ago and at the same time they are saving (in cash terms) very little. And the nature of how they borrow has changed. Now, the number of people cashing in on the equity based in their property has soared. Further advances on first mortgages alone have nearly doubled. Secured lending - or "lending large and lending long" - seems here to stay. The amount of revolving credit - most notably through credit cards - has risen sharply.

At the same time, some traditional forms of credit are less used. Hire purchase is now less popular, and some relatively expensive forms of small-scale credit like the tallyman and the discount cheque - have also declined in importance.

Mortgage credit

Much of the increase in lending secured against people's homes must itself result from the increase in wealth derived from wider home ownership and the increases in house prices. Through the increasing value of their homes, people have simply had more wealth and have been prepared to borrow using their homes as security.

In such a situation, it is clear that some of the increase in borrowing can ultimately be traced back to the highly favoured tax position of home ownership as against other forms of saving and investment, or indeed other forms of house tenure. Clearly the tax privileges result from a political decision to encourage people to own their own homes, supported by successive governments. However, as home ownership becomes ever more predominantly the major form of housing tenure, there does seem to be a need to consider the effect of tax privileges in increasing the total volume of consumer borrowing, especially since they apply to all home owners and not just to those on the first step of the ladder.

Credit casualties

In a sense, we can take the benefits of credit for granted. Most people have little difficulty getting credit if they want it. There are special problems about people on very low incomes, to which we return. However, much of the popular criticism of credit now is not that it is too hard to get, but that there is too much available.

It is therefore worth considering the evidence about the number and type of casualties among people who have been given credit but cannot manage it.

When we did the research for our 1980 report, we found that three per cent of our survey respondents had experienced problems with recent credit arrangements. A similar proportion had had problems some time over the previous five years. The Office of Fair Trading survey in 1987/88 found that ten per cent of their sample had some experience of repayment difficulties over the previous five years.

However, while credit use has risen dramatically, evidence indicates that it is the same people using *more* credit rather than a significant increase in *new* credit users that is largely responsible for the growth. This raises the possibility that it is not invariably the "credit novice" who gets into difficulties.

This ties in with the sort of cases presented to money advisers and debt counsellors - usually involving long-term multiple debt. It is this qualitative evidence that seems to point towards a change in the nature of personal indebtedness - involving multiple commitments. In 1981 there were an estimated 1.3 million households who could not meet their commitments; by 1987 this had risen to over 2 million. This absolute increase, combined with the changing quality of the debts, is a worrying development.

There have been very few full-scale studies from which to estimate the number of current casualties. The Policy Studies Institute is now carrying out a major research programme and a new and better estimate will, we hope, be one of its outcomes.

What evidence there is - debt judgements in court, for instance - suggests that while the number of people having difficulties has gone up, the rise has not matched the *overall* increase in the rate of borrowing. Various factors have contributed to the casualty rate - more marriage breakdowns, the recession, and associated unemployment, of the early 1980s and changes in the way creditors collect debts. But whatever the relationships between causes, the numbers are significant, and they are increasing. This clearly needs to be addressed. Moreover, people's debts are becoming more complex, reflecting the widening variety of different *types* of credit over the decade. All these factors combine to make it much easier for people to get into a serious financial muddle than ever before.

The advice services which deal with consumer problems are certainly increasingly anxious about debt difficulties.

However, it is hard to assert that the increased availability and use of credit have, in themselves, led to an increasing proportion of casualties.

What is true is that there has been a very marked increase in the number of homes repossessed because of difficulties with mortgage payments. The rise flattened out in 1988 only to go up again, by 29 per cent, in the second half of 1989. Again, though, the number of mortgage repossessions still only represents a tiny proportion of all people with mortgages.

However, there are - and always will be - people who ought only to have access to limited amounts of credit. There are two ways of dealing with this - not necessarily mutually exclusive: the government could impose restrictions, or lenders themselves could restrict how much they lend and to whom.

It appears that, as the credit market becomes more complex, it is harder for government to introduce restrictions that will be effective. This imposes a particular responsibility on lenders.

The National Consumer Council has always taken the view that consumers do not have a right to credit. It must be for the lender to take the responsible decision. In this, consumers and lenders have broadly the same interest. Consumers who can manage credit should be able to get it, and those who cannot should not. Lenders will not make money out of consumers who cannot repay their loans. We return later to the need for lenders to make the best possible judgements about the way they lend.

However sound the judgements made by lenders about the creditworthiness of borrowers, there are bound to be some occasions when consumers have difficulties in repaying. Systems in this country, both for collecting debts and for personal bankruptcy, are archaic. They need improving. In particular, debt enforcement methods need rationalising, to the benefit of all parties. In this respect, we are pleased to see that the recommendations of the Civil Justice Review have been included in the Courts and Legal Services Bill. We particularly support the proposed changes to the administration order which, if approved by parliament, will help those who have got into multiple debt to begin to sort out their repayment schedules.

Changing interest rates

Another characteristic of the last few years has been the large changes in the level of interest rates, particularly for mortgages. Essentially these have resulted from the government's use of interest rates as a tool of economic management to control inflation.

The considerable variations have placed great strains on mortgage borrowers. In periods when interest rates go up and down quite sharply, it is extremely difficult for consumers to assess their future commitments accurately.

One response has been to introduce new mortgage schemes, such as those offering lower rates of interest for new (as opposed to existing) borrowers; deferred interest loans; and new fixed-rate schemes, with interest rates ranging from 12.25 to 12.75 per cent (in April 1989). If mortgage interest rates are to continue to be so variable over the next few years, there will be pressure on the markets to continue to develop lending packages that guarantee more stable outgoings for consumers.

There is also a possible regulatory response. In the United States, it is common to have regulations which limit the possible increase in a variable interest rate for mortgages. The effect is to transfer some of the risks of large variations in interest rates from the borrower to the lender.

Information about credit costs

One of the great disappointments for consumer organisations over the last ten years has been the slowness with which consumers have made use of the information they are given about the relative costs of credit.

When we produced our report in 1980, very few people understood the annual percentage rate (APR). It had only recently been introduced and we hoped that consumers would learn to use it. The Office of Fair Trading research of 1987 shows that our hopes have not been fulfilled. The majority of people still do not understand APR - or know how to use it. Consumers concentrate on whether they can afford the periodic repayments of a particular loan and how easy it is for them to get it. They do not, on the whole, shop around sufficiently for the cheapest rate.

One consequence of this is, we believe, that charges for credit are generally higher than they need be. There is very little competitive pressure to bring down interest rates.

There are two possible types of response to this. One is education. The other is to highlight the relevant information so that consumers can be encouraged to seek out better credit buys and so induce lenders to compete for custom by offering lower rates. There are a number of ways in which this information could be emphasised.

More attention to real-life interest rate problems could be given in the school curriculum. Government agencies like the Office of Fair Trading could regularly publicise the different levels of interest rates being charged for different types of lending. Financial journalists could give more advice about Best Buys in borrowing.

Whatever is done, however, it is clear that it is still likely to be many years before most consumers are going to be able to make comparisons of the relative costs of credit in practice.

This makes it necessary at least to consider the regulatory approach to interest rates. In certain states in the United States and in some European countries it has been the practice to put legislative ceilings on rates for various types of lending. In the United States, for instance, legal restrictions on credit card interest rates are common. This approach has never been popular with regulators, nor indeed with consumer organisations, in this country. It is felt that any formal limit on interest rates laid down by regulation is likely to have one or other of three possible bad effects:

★ in order to be practical, the rate may have to be set so high as to have no effect in actual practice;

★ setting a top limit on interest rates may encourage lenders to set rates at or near the limit when they could be lower;

★ if the regulation is effective in limiting the interest that lenders would otherwise have charged, it must also to some extent ration the availability of credit. The likely consequence is that, at each point at which there is a limit, marginal consumers will be squeezed out; if they want credit, they will have to go to more expensive sources. In the worst cases, people desperate for money may be unable to get credit within the regulated systems at all and may end up going to illegal moneylenders.

These arguments will need to be reconsidered during the 1990s as the United Kingdom's systems come more and more into contact with those in the rest of Europe.

Whatever the outcome of the more general discussion, the National Consumer Council is convinced that there are some rates of interest which are so outrageous that they should not be allowed. In this country we have seen real rates of interest equal to fifty per cent on loans secured on people's homes and over one hundred per cent on some unsecured loans. We have suggested that the Director General of Fair Trading issue guidance from time to time about rates of interest that are high and cannot reasonably be justified.

Besides improving the information that consumers get before they take on credit, there is a crying need to improve the availability of money advice to individuals. The decisions that people have to take about the financial management of their lives are complex - and becoming more so. Those decisions can have very profound effects: decisions about personal pensions or about managing money in retirement can make very considerable differences to individual security and happiness. So can help for people facing a complex of debt problems. The need to improve the structures and funding of money advice will grow.

Encouraging new types of lender

One of the major problems with credit is that it is natural for those who are least able to afford high interest rates to have to pay them. People who have low incomes and no capital are worse risks. They therefore have to pay more than those who are better-off. However much we improve information to consumers and however responsible the practice of commercial credit-granters, this basic problem cannot be solved without going outside the operation of a normal credit market.

One way forward is the development of credit unions. In many countries credit unions have proved an extremely effective way for people on low incomes to get access to credit at a reasonable cost on a cooperative basis. However, their growth in this country has been very slow and uncertain. New and imaginative efforts need to be made to develop them.

Another possible way forward is the development of public institutions which provide credit where no market organisation could do so at a commercial cost. It is possible that the social fund, introduced by the present government, might become such an institution. Although, as we suggest later in the book, it is a form of lending that is highly unfriendly to its users at the moment, the social fund does provide a basis for development. It demonstrates that, if some people are to be able to borrow at all, they need a lender who will advance money on non-commercial terms. A similar role is played in some countries by municipal banks and other non-market institutions. Again, there seems room for imaginative developments here.

Improving credit-granting practice

We can seek to improve credit-granting practice. Lenders need to have the best information they can get if they are to lend responsibly. There is a sensitive tension between the need for lenders to have comprehensive information about potential borrowers and the rights of us all as individuals to privacy about our financial affairs. The National Consumer Council sees the best resolution of this tension in consumer choice.

The responsible exchange of information by lenders about individual capacity to repay should be encouraged, but we continue to believe that the terms on which lenders lend should be their responsibility. In this respect, they may wish to offer consumers the opportunity to choose whether or not private information about themselves as individuals should be passed on to third parties. Alternatively, lenders may decide to make this part of the terms of the agreement, merely informing the consumer that the information will be deposited with a licensed credit reference agency for the purposes of credit assessment. If lenders decide to take the latter course, other recommendations (in section 4) will ensure that consumers are kept informed and aware of the information that is being filed, with whom, and for what specific purpose. We hope too that, with time, a system of automatic access and checking will be offered to consumers.

As we have argued earlier, given the difficulties involved in government restraints on the availability of credit, lenders have a particular responsibility to see that credit is only granted prudently. We attach particular importance to two points:

★ lenders should give more weight, in their judgements about creditworthiness, to individuals' capacity to repay, rather than relying as much as they do now on past evidence of individuals' behaviour as borrowers;

★ as an encouragement to lenders to make the most prudent decisions, lenders should be able to enforce debts only if they can demonstrate that they have used appropriate sources of information about credit-worthiness. In fact, we believe all responsible lenders do now behave in this way: the effect of such a change in the law would be to bear down on those who lend extortionately or irresponsibly.

Conclusion

The rest of this book looks at trends in consumer credit and debt during the last ten years. Our recommendations - in section 5 - propose action points in the areas of: consumer information and advice about credit; risk assessment techniques; credit insurance; revolving credit; secured lending; low-income borrowers; creditors' default procedures; and court action against debtors.

Here we set a broader scene, by outlining some of the major areas for debate, as we see it, during the next ten years:

★ can consumers sustain or increase their current level of indebtedness without increasing the number of people who become casualties?

★ how, in particular, can we ensure that lending against the security of a home does not become extravagant?

★ how can we soften the impact on borrowers of sudden and frequent changes in interest rates?

★ how can we improve the systems for dealing with people who do become credit casualties?

★ how can we improve consumers' understanding of the relative costs of credit? And if we cannot, do we need to take other action to produce the competitive downward pressure on interest rates that informed consumer choice should bring?

★ how do we control outrageous overcharging for credit?

★ how do we provide better money advice structures?

★ can we encourage new types of lender for those consumers who are badly served by the way the commercial market works?

★ what improvements need to be made to credit-granting practice? In particular, how do we encourage the use of good credit referencing information while safeguarding personal privacy?

1. Personal borrowing: the facts and figures

Here we look at trends in the ten years since our 1979/80 review, *Consumers and Credit* (1). We start with information on "consumer wealth" - that is, personal disposable income, expenditure and savings, and assets.

These set the context for the figures on the levels of borrowing, which we look at in section 1.2. The official statistics in this area are scattered, and vary in quality and quantity. Changes in the way they are compiled and reported have made it difficult always to establish trends with accuracy. But within this constraint, we have divided the market, and the figures, into two broad areas, outlining the features of each and their relationship with each other. *Consumer credit* is one area, conventionally covering unsecured bank loans, overdrafts, credit cards, retail credit, finance house lending, insurance company loans, mail order and other money lending. *Borrowing for house purchase* is the other area.

In section 1.3 we look briefly at other forms of borrowing such as loans from credit unions and the social fund and - a significant, though often ignored source of borrowing - the postponed payment of rent, fuel and telephone bills, sometimes called "proxy credit".

The tables referred to in this and subsequent chapters are grouped together in the appendices at the end of the book.

1.1 Consumer wealth

High inflation and relatively limited access to credit characterised the 1970s. With rapidly rising prices making it sensible to buy now, pay later, consumer demand for credit began to grow.

In the 1980s - a period largely of falling inflation - the demand for credit strengthened, with a shift in the overall economic circumstances of Britain's households that significantly fuelled demand.

1.1.1 INCOME AND EXPENDITURE

Between 1986 and 1988 real personal disposable income rose by almost 8 per cent - a very rapid growth rate. Average earnings were expected to increase by a further 9 per cent-plus until late 1990.

The impact on consumer spending has been marked. In the United Kingdom, consumption has been growing 25 per cent faster than gross national product, far outstripping, for example, Japan or the United States. See Table I.1 *Real disposable income and real consumers' expenditure, 1982-88* (in appendix I).

1.1.2 SAVINGS

Inflation fell in the years after 1983, only recently starting an upward curve. That fall, combined with the rise in personal disposable income, might have been expected to lead to an *increase* in savings. But on the contrary, the amount of personal disposable income saved by individuals has *dropped* steadily over the decade. This is measured by what is called the "savings ratio" - the difference between what people have to spend after tax (that is, disposable income) and what they appear to spend (consumer expenditure). In 1989 it was at its lowest level for thirty years, at 4.8 per cent compared to 13.8 per cent in 1980. See Table I.2 *Outstanding consumer credit, inflation rate and savings ratio 1979-88* and Table I.3 *Personal sector income and expenditure 1979-88*.

This aspect of consumer behaviour - an apparent disinclination to save cash - has puzzled many commentators. It may be attributable to the preceding inflation-haunted years of the 1970s, when people could see little value in saving. It may also reflect the deregulation of financial markets and the sudden dramatic increase in the availability of credit. The answer probably lies in a combination of many factors influencing people to spend their cash and to invest in non-cash items, notably houses.

On the face of it, the fall in personal savings combined with the dramatic rise in outstanding credit (discussed below) also hints at family and individual overcommitment. There has been some debate about how the savings ratio is calculated (2, 3 and 4) and it may be that the level of borrowing distorts the real ratio of household spending.

1.1.3 OTHER ASSETS

Savings may also have been transferred to less liquid investments like property and pensions.

Life assurance and pension fund payments, as a proportion of household spending, increased over the ten years up to 1989. In 1979 they accounted for 2.5 per cent of expenditure of total disposable household income. By 1987 this had reached 6 per cent. However, this may have been an effect of the switch from annuity to endowment mortgages that followed the introduction of mortgage interest relief at source (MIRAS) in 1983.

Share-ownership has also grown, from almost 7 per cent of the adult population in 1979 to just over 20 per cent by 1988. But although around one in five adults now owns shares, a recent analysis (5) shows that income from shares and dividends only contributes significantly in the highest-earning households. People in the lower- and middle-income brackets tend to get a higher percentage of unearned income from the relatively uncomplicated and accessible building society account. Similarly, the higher-income person gets proportionately more unearned income from property.

Indeed the largest proportion of capital in the UK is tied up in property. Overall it accounts for the bulk of household wealth. The proportion of owner-occupiers has risen steadily for almost forty years, with only a brief interruption during the second world war. In 1988 65 per cent of UK homes were owner-occupied, higher than many other European countries: the most recent figures for West Germany, Switzerland and Sweden, for example, show around 40 per cent owner-occupation. (Section 1.3 looks at borrowing for house purchase and in section 2 we discuss the demographic perspective of property ownership.)

So in the mid-to-late 1980s, consumers overall had more personal disposable income, they saved less, and they spent more. Much of their increased expenditure was, as we shall now see, financed by borrowing.

1.2 Consumer credit

1.2.1 THE SUPPLIERS AND THE VOLUME

There was a marked, steady rise in the volume of credit commitments taken on by consumers during the 1980s.

The largest share of the unsecured credit market is with the monetary sector (explained in the box). The average growth for the overall consumer credit sector has been around 18 per cent a year. Within this, credit card lending has grown particularly fast. Table I.4 gives *the monetary sector's credit and house purchase loans for 1979-88 in £billion.*

THE MONETARY SECTOR

This term covers: the UK offices of all institutions authorised to take deposits under the Banking Act 1987 - largely the high street banks; the banking department of the Bank of England; those institutions in the Channel Islands and the Isle of Man that have opted to conform with the monetary control arrangements introduced in August 1981; and, prior to their recognition as banks, National Girobank and the Trustees Savings Banks.

Monthly statistics are generally only collected from those members of the monetary sector with "eligible liabilities" of £10 million or more or "total liabilities" of £100 million or more - in other words, the larger institutions.

More recently, one of the fastest growing sectors has been lending by finance houses, which are partly responsible for underwriting retail credit card operations.

With the greater flexibility allowed to them by the 1986 Building Societies Act, unsecured lending by building societies has also grown rapidly. It remains to be seen whether this will continue in the early 1990s.

Credit cards

There has been a remarkable rise in the number of credit cards in circulation, and a widespread instinct that this has been responsible for the 1980s consumer spending boom.

In 1979 credit cards accounted for just under 10 per cent of non-mortgage outstanding credit. In 1988, this had risen to about 16 per cent. The number of issued bank cards alone tripled in ten years, from 8 million in 1978 to over 25 million by 1988.

However, in terms of credit outstanding on bank cards, the fastest spurt seems to have been in the early years of the decade, with a growth rate of around 30 per cent a year between 1980 and 1985, slowing to 11 per cent by 1988. In 1989 bank cards accounted for only 16 per cent of the consumer credit market.

There has been a general increase in the number of borrowers who pay their monthly statements in full, and so incur no interest charges. Barclaycard estimate that around 46 per cent of their cardholders pay no charges. Other banks, including Girobank, have even higher numbers, some approaching 65 per cent.

Figures for repayments on retail credit cards vary between suppliers, and probably reflect the socio-economic profiles of their customers. Fifty per cent of Marks and Spencer card users avoid paying interest charges compared to 30 per cent of Storecard users.

Overall then, credit card commitments account for only a minor share of the total personal borrowing market and the ratio of outstanding credit to turnover has been falling slowly, from 0.45 in 1979 to 0.31 in 1988.

1.2.2 FINANCE HOUSE LENDING

Finance houses vary enormously in size and in origin. Many of the largest are subsidiaries of the major clearing banks, originally set up to meet the demand for credit for car purchase: these include Mercantile Credit (owned by Barclays Bank), Forward Trust (by Midland Bank) and Lloyds Bowmaker (by Lloyds Bank). Others have their origins in business leasing and consumer hire purchase services.

By the mid-1980s the 47 members of the Finance Houses Association (FHA) accounted for over 80 per cent of all finance house lending in the UK: we therefore use their figures to give a snapshot of the changes in this sector over the past decade.

Between 1979 and 1988 the volume of outstanding credit granted by FHA members to consumers rose from 32.4 to 38.6 per cent. (See Table I.5 *Changes in credit business of FHA members, 1979-88.*) When we turn to *new* credit, the trend is more dramatic.

In less than ten years up to 1987, new consumer lending by FHA members moved from being one-third of all their new lending to over a half. Within the financial sector, institutions lending to consumers have become more dominant and profitable. External factors enabled this, including the lifting of controls on hire purchase in July 1982: this boosted sales in the used car market, and had a related effect in other areas.

There was a slight cutback in the growth of consumer lending in 1988. The FHA reported a downturn in the last quarter of 1988, although lending rose overall. Most affected was the new and used car finance sector (their traditional business base), following the rise in interest rates in autumn 1988. Table I.6 categorises *the purposes for which new credit was extended by FHA members from 1984 to 1988.*

The changing focus can be assessed in various ways. The expertise and origin of new entrants into the credit market have changed, in line with the membership base of the FHA. It may be a rapid response to consumer demand - especially for loans for house purchase and revolving credit: these are two major growth areas in the finance houses sector, as Table I.6 makes clear. It is likely that there has been a knock-on effect in second mortgage lending for home improvements - another growth area of the decade: new lending for home improvements rose steadily in volume, although its proportionate share has been overshadowed by the growth in loans for home purchase. See Table I.7 *FHA lending for home improvements and property, 1985-88.*

1.2.3 INSURANCE COMPANIES

While insurance companies have increased their consumer lending, they have generally done so at a slower rate than other lenders and most of the recent growth has been for home loans. See Table I.8 *Insurance companies: growth in consumer credit outstanding, 1979-87.*

Insurance companies have traditionally served the higher-income borrower, with larger loans than other types of lender. Their position as a leading source of bridging loans and top-up mortgages appears to have been breached by competition from the banks, driving insurance companies to diversify into new forms of lending.

While it is not possible to separate out the figures, remortgaging and equity lending appear to be growing. With this type of loan, home owners may be offered up to 90 per cent of the value of their property (85 per cent if the house is worth over £80,000). While standard (and competitive) interest rates are offered, some insurance companies also offer a variable rate according to the size of the loan (the larger the loan, the lower the annual percentage rate).

This area of lending is likely to grow further. The trend into owner-occupation, combined with an ageing population and substantial inheritances of parental homes, will bring about a larger group of asset-rich households. The credit needs of older people are very different from those of younger age groups. And the security they offer to lenders is greater. This makes them an increasingly attractive target for new lending services and products. We discuss this further in section 2.

1.2.4 RETAIL GROUPS

Shops have accounted for a significant increase in consumer credit - a rise of over 50 per cent since 1981 - and in late-1989 accounted for around 7 per cent of outstanding consumer credit. See Table I.9 *New retail credit extended and retail credit outstanding, 1979-88.*

The Finance Houses Association figures (discussed in section 1.2.2) include some retail group lending: member institutions may be part of, or own, large retail operations or have influential retail groups as customers. See Table I.10 *FHA member companies and their customers, 1987/88.* In 1988 the Burton group had 25 per cent of the retail credit market. Marks and Spencer's credit card, operating through just one retail chain, had a 14 per cent share, only 1 per cent less than the Club 24 group with its multiple outlets. This sector grew at about 16 per cent a year over five years up to 1989, compared to 8 per cent for charge cards and 11 per cent for bank credit cards.

Until the recent evidence of a slow-down in consumer spending, retailers seemed set to expand further with the introduction of new multi-service financial packages tied to their credit card operations. In any event, competition in the high street feeds the incentive to develop cross-selling. In this context, the information about customers gathered through the use of retail credit cards is an increasingly valuable commodity to suppliers - an issue on which the National Consumer Council has already expressed concern (6).

Credit for home improvements

An interesting development within the retail market is linked to the rise in mortgages and home improvement loans - the fast rise in do-it-yourself retail sales. Official figures tend to leave out purchases like paint and wallpaper, power tools and garden equipment. But the Office of Fair Trading survey of 1987 (7) into consumers' use of credit showed that credit was commonly used to pay for home improvement items.

It is worth considering the effect of DIY and home furnishing purchases on demand for credit, the use to which that credit is put, and the effect of owner-occupation in inflating demand.

A recent market research study (8) has shown that, if the officially excluded items are added in, DIY retail sales have increased much faster than total consumer spending (they rose by 16 per cent between 1980 and

1986, accelerated in 1987, and only slowly began to stabilise towards the middle of 1988). See Table I.11 *Do-it-yourself spending by volume, 1980-86, two estimates*.

Moreover, DIY sales show a close relationship with house price inflation. The study revealed that DIY-type expenditure was particularly high in London and the south-east.

The Office of Fair Trading survey also shows that the south-east has the heaviest use of credit cards, charge cards, mortgages and bank overdrafts, and the lowest number of non-users of credit.

There has been a proliferation of large plant hire and multi-purpose DIY "warehouses" (such as Sainsbury's Homebase stores). Many of these offer their own credit cards - W H Smith market a Do-It-All credit card and MFI and Harris Queensway offer personal credit card services - with the funds provided by finance houses.

While the precise links between DIY sales, home ownership, credit demand and use need more detailed statistical evidence, it seems realistic to assume an association. We refer to this topic again in sections 2 and 3.

1.2.5 BUILDING SOCIETIES - LOANS FOR PURPOSES OTHER THAN HOUSE PURCHASE

Since the Building Societies Act 1986, companies with assets of more than £100 million have been able to offer personal loans, overdrafts and credit cards. These are some of the most profitable services in the financial services sector. While moving rapidly to offer credit cards and personal loans, the large building societies cautiously offered them initially to existing customers only. This may enable them to operate with a lower risk of bad debt and default in a traditionally high-risk lending sector.

Many building societies have also introduced *new* secured loan services - again reducing the associated risk by offering them predominantly to existing borrowers. Examples are the Halifax Xtraloan, Bradford & Bingley's Flexiloan and the Woolwich Multiloan. Loans secured against people's homes are offered for periods of between three and twenty-five years, at very competitive interest rates (16 to 18 per cent APR in 1989).

Some of the largest building societies, including Halifax and (until its conversion to plc status in 1989) Abbey National, are lending their own funds up to a maximum of £10,000 to existing customers (in 1989, raised from the earlier £5,000 limit in February 1988). Others operate as agents for larger lenders. The National & Provincial, Britannia and Cheshire Building Societies act as agents for the FHA member North West Securities (which in turn is a subsidiary of the Bank of Scotland).

Statistics on unsecured lending by building societies were still limited at the time of writing, but they appear to show a rising custom for this source of credit. A 61 per cent rise in new advances in the second quarter of 1988 was followed by a further 31 per cent rise in the third quarter - a higher rate of increase than any other sector. Moreover, some building societies are now offering unsecured loans to non-customers. This is likely to increase.

While it is not uncommon for initial demand for a new product to be high, it will be interesting to see if the growth rate is sustained. It will undoubtedly be affected by the change in status of the Abbey National plc.

One of the major features of building society lending has been the increasing importance of *further advances on existing mortgages* - ostensibly for home improvements and repairs which were formerly eligible for tax relief. See Table I.12 *Further advances on existing mortgages, 1979-87.*

1.2.6 THE HIGH STREET BANKS AND THE MONETARY SECTOR

Lending by the monetary sector (largely the high street banks - see the box in section 1.2.1 for further details) increased steadily during the 1980s; in December 1988, 65 per cent of outstanding consumer credit not for mortgages was bank lending, and around 16 per cent was on bank credit cards. Outstanding credit on bank cards has more than tripled. See Table I.13 *Consumer credit outstanding, by sector.* However, the existence of "free riders" using credit cards (that is, people who regularly pay their accounts in full and incur no interest charges) may produce an overestimate of outstanding credit commitment. (See the note on page 98.)

As well as lending more for house purchase, the banks have developed their secured lending market by introducing new products. For example, Midland Bank offer their home-owning customers the HomeOwners' Reserve, a revolving account that gives fifty times a monthly payment, up to £15,000. Barclays Bank offer Homeowner Loans, with a limit of £50,000 secured on property, with long repayment periods. Lloyds Bank's Home-stretcher personal loan is similar. Until the 1988 spring budget, most of these loans attracted tax relief making them a doubly attractive proposition.

Unsecured personal loans from banks and building societies, overdrafts, finance house loans, mail order, hire purchase, moneylending, check trading and other licensed lenders cumulatively represent around £42.8 billion of outstanding credit. The vast majority of this - 80 per cent - is lending by the monetary sector. The rest - around £8.4 billion of outstanding credit - is by non-monetary credit companies, insurance companies and retailers (1988 figures).

1.3 Borrowing for home purchase

Buying a home is usually the largest single purchase made by most consumers. And in the 1980s, even more dramatic than the rise in credit acquired for goods and services was the leap in borrowing to buy a home.

By 1984, for the monetary sector, the level of outstanding loans for mortgages matched that for consumer credit, and has subsequently outstripped it. See Table I.14 *Monetary sector: ratio of outstanding lending on consumer credit agreements and lending for house purchase, 1979-87.*

By the end of 1988 the total lent as mortgages was £225 billion. The average rise was around 20 per cent a year, with sharper rises in 1981/2,

1985/6 and 1987/88. See Table I.15 *Changes in home loans market: debt outstanding, 1979-88*. In 1987 and 1988 gross mortgage advances by building societies alone rose by 51 per cent, and net new commitments by 54 per cent.

We now look at how total mortgage borrowing is divided between the various types of lender. Table I.16 shows *the source of mortgage or loan by socio-economic group of head of household, 1986.*

1.3.1 THE BUILDING SOCIETIES

Among the top ten mortgage lenders, which between them accounted for 61 per cent of loans for house purchase by the first quarter of 1988, eight were building societies (the remaining two were banks). See Table I.17 *The ten major mortgage lenders and their market shares, 1988.*

Building societies, by far the most significant mutual savings and loans institutions in the UK, have been getting fewer in number, and larger in size, since the start of the century. This trend has been particularly marked in recent years.

The number of building societies fell by a third between 1960 and 1970 and by another 43 per cent between 1970 and 1980. The reduction has been just as steep since 1980, with a large number of mergers, especially among the smaller regional societies. 1986 saw the largest ever building society merger - between the Nationwide and Anglia Building Societies: at the time they accounted for around 14 per cent of the industry's assets between them.

By the end of 1987 there were only 118 registered societies and the Building Societies Association estimates that, judging by the 1986 rate of decline, there could be fewer than 50 societies by 1995 (9 and 10). The numbers of borrowers and of shareholders have meanwhile been rising.

The entry of banks into the home loans market hit directly at the building societies' traditional business. By the first quarter of 1987, the building societies market share had slipped to 60 per cent, and went on falling before a slight upturn at the end of the year. Because of a sharp rise in the level of repayments of principal during 1987, building society figures for *net* lending show an even more marked fall. Their market share fell to just 50 per cent. For the last six months of 1987, building societies were responsible for only 46 per cent of *new lending*.

This loss of market share has had substantial and far-reaching effects. It has driven the building societies, and notably the top twenty societies with their giant's share of the total building society market, to diversify into new products and services. The increase in the size of building societies, and their reduction in numbers, puts them in a strong position to challenge the banks' dominance of retail banking services and also to influence the development of other markets, notably unsecured consumer credit. (At the time of writing, the effect of the conversion of Abbey National to plc status on the distribution of resources and market share was not yet clear.)

The shifts in market share have also had an impact on the lending portfolios of both building societies and other creditors, especially in the profile of first-time buyers and other new borrowers. This is examined again in section 2.

1.3.2 THE HIGH STREET BANKS

The seventeen-fold increase in net lending for house purchase by the monetary sector - largely the high street banks - since 1979 demonstrates their speedy penetration of the market. Bank subsidiaries loaned a further £1,568 million for house purchase in 1987. See Table I.18 *Net lending for house purchase by the monetary sector, 1979-87.*

By early 1988 two banks - Lloyds and Barclays - had joined the building societies among the top ten mortgage lenders, with 3.7 per cent and 3.4 per cent shares respectively (see Table I.17).

In fact the banks had captured, and were consolidating, much of the home loans market by 1987. Although about a third of their lending was to first-time buyers, over half of these loans were for more than £30,000, and nearly half were for homes costing more than £50,000 compared to a quarter of equivalent building society loans.

The banks' more prosperous customer base is reflected in the smaller advances in proportion to prices paid for properties, averaging 56 per cent. By contrast, building societies made an average 70 per cent advance in proportion to price, and other lenders up to and over 95 per cent. See Table I.19 *Average prices of houses and average advances, by lending source, 1981-88.* One major effect of the steep rise in monetary sector mortgage lending has been to push other lenders towards higher-risk borrowers.

The entry of the banks into the home loans market has also given a strong competitive edge to the cross-selling of other financial products and packages - life and home insurance, pensions, home equity plans and, significantly, other credit services.

1.3.3 THE INSURANCE COMPANIES AND PENSION FUNDS

The insurance companies' traditional customer base was among older, more affluent borrowers - people who were often looking for a topping-up loan rather than complete funding of a house purchase. They have always made higher than average advances and for more expensive properties.

In the mid-1980s, insurance companies, like the building societies, began to feel the effects of the strengthening competition from the high street banks, and there was a fall in their new lending (see Table I.16). Since 1984 bank advances as a proportion of price of property have been consistently higher than insurance company advances. See Table I.19.

Lending by insurance companies is usually tied to an endowment mortgage, with the capital loan repaid at the end of the mortgage period from the proceeds of an endowment insurance policy on the borrower's life. In 1983 mortgage interest relief at source was introduced. Net lending by insurance companies went up by nearly 2,000 per cent, from £6 million in 1982 to £124 million in 1983, largely through borrowers switching from annuity to endowment mortgages.

Another factor affecting the popularity of insurance company home loans has been the tax relief on endowment policies. In April 1989 this was cut to the lower limit of 12.5 per cent.

Nevertheless, insurance companies remain an important source of funds for the more expensive house purchase and the better-off borrower, and may become more so in the trend towards home equity loans and refinancing for older, wealthier owner-occupiers.

1.3.4 THE LOCAL AUTHORITIES

Although their new lending and outstanding credit have been falling over the decade, local authorities hold a significant place in the market - providing most of their loans to enable council tenants to buy their homes. They have tended to meet the needs of higher-risk, lower-income borrowers, and to give a proportionately higher advance, as measured against income, than other lenders, on lower-priced property and at lower interest rates (although purchases below market value can distort the data on both average prices and the incomes of first-time buyers). Nevertheless, as Table I.16 shows, building societies are still overwhelmingly the principal source of mortgage credit for lower-income consumers.

1.3.5 OTHER FINANCIAL INSTITUTIONS

A growing variety of financial institutions other than the traditional ones now offer mortgages for homes. Although their combined total market share is small, in terms both of target market and size of loan, they are gradually becoming more significant - first mortgage lending by finance houses, for instance.

Lending by these other financial institutions is also largely responsible for the development in the UK of the *secondary mortgage* market (not to be confused with second mortgages. The *primary* market is the mortgage agreements between home purchasers and the original lenders. The *secondary* market buys up mortgages, repackages them as 'mortgage-backed securities' and sells them on to investors. See (11), for more about this market.)

Still small in the UK, the secondary mortgage market is substantial in the United States. There, financial restrictions mean that savings institutions have to borrow short-term at variable rates but lend long-term at fixed rates. The secondary mortgage market allows them to sell on their loans, so raising their liquidity and their ability to lend more.

In the UK, the building societies' need to diversify and expand in the face of sharpening competition has led them into the secondary mortgage market, although so far only cautiously, using mainly overseas funding to set up and service loans. That they have entered at all reflects the changes taking place within and between lenders in the home loans sector.

1.4 Other sources of personal borrowing

1.4.1 CREDIT UNIONS

Building societies, cooperative societies and trades unions are all registered as "friendly societies" - mutual organisations that may provide insurance, savings and loans and some other, limited, benefits to their members. In 1979 the Credit Unions Act provided for the registration, as friendly societies, of another institution relevant to our discussion - credit unions.

Credit union savings and loans funds are still minuscule in this country and play an insignificant role in the overall UK consumer credit market. Nevertheless, they provide a service for a minority of borrowers. We discuss the potential for their development below.

By November 1988, there were 241 credit unions in the UK. Of these, the 99 Northern Ireland credit unions are, by and large, older and wealthier and have more members than the British ones. The average membership per credit union in 1986 was 1,240 in Northern Ireland, compared to 280 in the rest of the United Kingdom. Average assets were £532,800 in Northern Ireland and £72,260 for the rest and average total loans £428,620 in Northern Ireland compared to £62,870 for the rest. See Table I.20 *Credit unions in Northern Ireland and Great Britain 1986.*

In fact, these averages disguise huge variations between individual credit unions, both in Northern Ireland and in Britain. Table I.21 shows the variations in assets and loans, by numbers of members.

Lending policies also seem to vary between regions. In Northern Ireland in 1988 the average loan to members was over £200, but less than £1,000. In Britain there was more variation: fourteen credit unions averaged less than £200 per loan while three averaged more than £1,000.

The members of each union must be linked by a definable "common bond", such as living in one identifiable neighbourhood or working for one employer. A recent survey (12) found a good occupational mix within seven different kinds of credit union. However, the common bond requirement means that members tend to be recruited from a clearly defined and homogeneous group. So one credit union, based in a London suburb, has a large majority of professional and managerial members, with average available incomes of over £110 a week, who are buying or already own their homes. In marked contrast is a Scottish credit union where half the members are unemployed, almost two-thirds have available incomes of less than £10 a week, and all are tenants.

Despite their tiny share in the national consumer credit cake, credit unions offer intriguing possibilities in small savings and loans at a local level in a period when building societies are increasingly distancing themselves from their origins as mutual savings-based friendly societies.

1.4.2 THE SOCIAL FUND

A formal, non-commercial credit source aimed at those in most need was created in April 1988. The government's social fund, which replaced the single payments scheme for supplementary benefits claimants, provides a system of discretionary no-interest credit in the form of cash loans.

Successful applicants may borrow between £30 and £1,000. The maximum repayment period is 78 weeks. Repayments are deducted directly from the claimant's income support, at a rate of up to 15 per cent of weekly benefit.

Loans are made at the discretion of individual benefit offices, each of which works to an annual cash limit on loans. (See (13) for a detailed examination of the scheme.)

The former single payments system cost £140 million in 1983 and over £300 million in 1985.

Take-up under the social fund loans scheme was initially low. In its first year of operation, £143 million was allocated for loans and £60 million for grants. After five months, expenditure was £50 million - only one quarter of the budget for the year. However, at the time of writing, the 1989 figures were showing a substantial increase. There are reports of heavy demand for grants and loans. In many cases, the cash limits had already been reached well before the end of the year.

We explore the trends in take-up of social fund borrowing in more detail in section 2.2.1.

1.4.3 INFORMAL SOURCES OF CREDIT

Moving away from official statistics, there are various other important forms of borrowing not usually included in figures for total consumer credit and home loans. These include loans from charities and from friends and relatives. Interestingly, only 2 per cent of the 1987 Office of Fair Trading survey respondents spontaneously mentioned these sources of credit, and the number borrowing in this way was under 1 per cent, mostly younger people.

Quantitatively more significant is the "proxy credit" people obtain by delaying payment on their fuel, power and rent commitments. Nearly all households use these measures once in a while when they are temporarily overcommitted (or forgetful) and they are used more often by households whose commitments have become unmanageable. Figures are only available for those who have run into real difficulty - people who are in arrears, or who are disconnected or evicted. Because this is essentially an incomplete and negative side of consumer credit, we give the facts and figures for this type of "borrowing", and explore them in their wider context, in section 2.5.

References to section 1

1. National Consumer Council, *Consumers and Credit*, NCC, 1980.
2. Steven Bell, "How savings statistics were mismeasured", *Financial Times*, 8 August 1988, p.11

3. David Fleming, *Time for a Realistic Measure of Savings*, discussion paper no. 3, Cadogan Management Ltd, March 1989.

4. Mark Franklin and others, "Why has UK personal saving collapsed?", *CSFB Economics*, Credit Suisse First Boston, July 1989.

5. "The effects of taxes and benefits on household income, 1986" *Economic Trends* no. 422, December 1988, pp. 89-99.

6. National Consumer Council, *Taking Liberties: commercial use of personal financial information*, NCC, PD16/88, May 1988.

7. PAS Business Surveys for the Office of Fair Trading, *Omnibus Survey*, 1989.

8. Verdict Research Ltd, *Verdict on DIY by Retailers*, July 1987, cited in Spencer, Peter, "UK house prices - not an inflation signal", *CSFB Economics*, Credit Suisse First Boston, September 1987.

9. Building Societies Association, *Building Society Fact Book 1987*, BSA, 1988, p.6.

10. Building Societies Association, *Building Society Fact Book 1988*, BSA, 1989, p.6.

11. Mark Boleat, *New Lenders and the Secondary Mortgage Market*, Building Societies Association, 1988.

12. Richard Berthoud and Teresa Hinton, *Credit Unions in the United Kingdom*, Policy Studies Institute, 1989.

13. National Consumer Council, *The Social Fund*, unpublished paper, December 1988.

14. "Budget pressures threaten benefits", *The Observer*, July 1989, p.8.

2. Behind the facts: the influences on supply, demand, access and attitudes

In section 1 we looked at the figures for the supply and take-up of consumer credit - in its widest sense - in the ten years up to 1990. It was a time of huge shifts - when rises in the total amount of credit and the ways in which it was supplied were paralleled by accelerating consumer demand. In this section we discuss the various influences - economic, legal, fiscal and social - that underlie the facts and figures and that helped to shape the trends.

2.1 The supply of credit: deregulation of financial services

The deregulation of financial services in the 1980s overturned controls on bank lending and gave consumers wider choice and more access to a variety of credit services.

When we were researching our 1980 report, *Consumers and Credit*, house prices had started to surge after a period of recession. Inflation resurfaced and people began to reaffirm their faith in bricks and mortar, so the demand for home loans was high.

Consumers aiming to buy their own home turned almost automatically to the building societies, which then dominated the market for personal mortgages. However, the building societies operated a cartel in lending and deposit rates: they offered cheap loans but these were, in effect, rationed by a ceiling on the rates paid to depositors.

At the same time, a Bank of England rule held bank deposit interest rates at 9.5 per cent, and so artificially maintained the appeal of building society deposit accounts over those of the banks. This compounded the effect of the building society cartel and stifled competition in the supply of home loans.

One of the first activities of the new government in 1979 was to begin deregulation - ending the artificial rationing of mortgages that had distorted the housing market. The building societies' anti-competitive cartel was abolished and the Bank of England untied the "corset" on bank interest and lending. The banks became free to compete with building societies.

In early 1980 this released a huge backlog of demand for home loans. There was a dramatic increase in mortgage lending by new institutions - notably the high street banks - and the competition to recruit new borrowers sharpened. Despite the subsequent dip into economic recession, by 1982 the banks had captured 36 per cent of the market, and the traditional mortgage lenders were also fighting off further competition from insurance companies, finance houses and other, more specialist lenders.

Commercial necessity drove the building societies in particular, and financial institutions in general, to diversify into new credit services. This was fuelled by the lifting of hire purchase control in July 1982 and the growing demand for credit cards - all pointing the way to a profitable expansion in consumer lending.

In 1986 massive technological changes to its own systems by the City shortly preceded the implementation of the Financial Services Act: the effects on the financial services industry were near-revolutionary. The Building Societies Act 1986 recognised the need to allow building societies to compete on more equal terms with the banks, enabling them to offer customers a wider range of personal financial services, such as personal loans, overdrafts and credit cards, plus more specialised personal equity plans and pensions. Building societies still suffered from continuing controls on the funds upon which they were allowed to draw, although this too changed in 1988, when they were permitted to increase the proportion of funds raised from sources other than their investment customers. This went some way to recapture some of their lost market share.

For the first time for over a decade, the availability of loans was no longer a problem. The industry positively competed for first-time buyers and new credit users. Tax concessions were available on home mortgages and loans for home improvements (both amended in the March 1988 budget). More money was available from the wholesale (non-consumer) markets and was passed on in the form of improved access to personal borrowers. Table II.1 *Consumer credit and other personal sector borrowing outstanding, 1980-88* shows the extent and speed of the increase.

2.2 Consumers' demand for credit: influences in the 1980s

2.2.1 THE EFFECTS OF LEGISLATION

Perhaps the most significant legislative changes to affect the overall demand for loans were in the field of housing.

The Housing Act of 1980 gave local authority tenants a right to buy their homes and, four years later, the Housing and Building Control Act 1984 reduced the period within which tenants became eligible to buy and increased the discount for sitting tenants. Incentives to buy into various council house schemes, combined with demographic changes (discussed in section 2.2.3) and the fall in the amount of accommodation for rent from private landlords, all pushed up the demand for mortgages.

From the early 1970s, rent controls, the security of tenure regulations and soaring house prices meant that renting out became less and less attractive for private property owners. It was more profitable to sell. This trend was reinforced by the preferential tax treatment available to owner-occupiers buying on a mortgage (see the next section). Today only about 10 per cent of Britain's total housing is privately rented, a large share of this in London.

In addition, there are simply more households in Britain than there were. This follows changes in the population's age structure (see section 2.2.3), but has been boosted by other factors, including legislation.

The Matrimonial and Family Proceedings Act 1984 allowed a couple to petition for divorce after the first anniversary of their marriage. Before this people had to wait three years. The number of divorces rose by 6 per cent the following year. Britain has the highest divorce rate in the European Community - 12.9 for every 1,000 existing marriages in England and Wales (1986 figure).

The effect of marriage and divorce figures on the demand for credit are complex but potent. They certainly affect the rate at which new households are formed, particularly in the mid-age groups, and therefore the demand for accommodation and home loans. Furthermore, debt has long been associated with relationship breakdown - both as a catalyst of family problems and an effect of the formidable costs involved in separation and divorce.

Another legislative change with a bearing on consumer demand was the 1986 Social Security Act which introduced complex and far-reaching changes to the system of income-related benefits and to the structure and level of pensions. The Act was not fully implemented until April 1988.

We have already mentioned the initially low take-up of social fund interest-free loans. These were introduced in 1988, replacing non-refundable single payments - or outright grants. In the first year of its operation, take-up was so much lower than the previous take-up of lump sum outright grants that it raised the question: what happened to the demand once met by social security grants? These were predominantly made to families with children who, as we see later, are the group most likely to use credit. Subsequently, while we were writing this report, the rate at which people applied for, and were granted, loans altered substantially.

The initially low take-up led to the conclusion that many families who needed and were entitled to loans were simply not applying for them. Research showed a low level of awareness of the scheme and that people who did know about it were worried about being able to meet the repayments. A Scottish study of housing benefit claimants found that nearly two-thirds of them had applied for single payments under the old scheme and that 90 per cent of these were granted. Under the new social fund scheme, only 15 per cent of the same people had applied for a loan, of which only 50 per cent were granted. This represented a drop in demand of 76 per cent in one year (1).

The study found that almost half of the housing benefit claimants were reluctant to take on a loan or to get into debt. Many also believed that they would not qualify - not an unnatural assumption, perhaps, given the refusal rate.

There are other features of the social fund loan system that make it unfriendly as a source of credit. Applicants have to undergo a personal interview that is sometimes lengthy and occasionally within earshot of other applicants. As a form of credit, it is neither flexible nor convenient. Repayments are up to 15 per cent of social security benefit over eighteen months - a large slice of the household budget for people with incomes already heavily committed. And the repayments are automatically deducted at source, leaving no flexibility to juggle repayments according to need. In very low-income families, any *loan* - as opposed to an outright grant - inevitably operates as a straight cut in the weekly budget.

In section 3.4, we discuss how borrowers weigh up the costs of their credit. The initially low take-up of the interest-free social fund loan gave some useful pointers on this: clearly, consumers do not assess credit by its costs alone.

However, the level of applications for loans has now improved. This has been achieved not by improving the way the scheme operates but by publicising it more widely. By autumn 1989, government figures showed that over 500,000 people had had an interest-free loan, averaging £214. Expenditure on social fund loans was £125 million.

However, while 90 per cent of applications for "crisis loans" were granted, fears have been expressed that many priority groups - such as homeless families - are losing out on loans. Forty-one per cent of applications for "budgeting loans", often for items like bedding, carpets or cooking utensils, were refused. A small proportion of applicants were also turned down because loan officers judged that they would not be able to repay a loan (2). All these people would have to seek help elsewhere.

So in June 1988, while social fund officers were being urged by the Department of Social Security to be "more generous", and less rigid in interpreting the rules, figures were already emerging to show that loans made were running ahead of budget projections. Some offices were reported to be more than 40 per cent over their projected monthly budgets (3). This is particularly crucial in view of the fact that overspending in one month comes out of the following month's budget. If the overspending continues and monthly budgets dwindle, fewer and fewer applicants will be granted loans, and the loans will be smaller.

The principle of providing "social loans" to the least well-off is, we believe, a good one. We have serious doubts, however, about the social fund as it operates now being the most appropriate way of doing it. In section 5, we discuss some remedies.

2.2.2 TAXATION AND THE DEMAND FOR CREDIT

There have long been fiscal incentives to use credit, most particularly for the purchase and improvement of homes. Some of these are complex, such as the relief available on secured loans taken out to buy annuities for people over sixty-five. Others, such as exemption from capital gains tax and mortgage interest tax relief, are better known and understood. Most influential in recent years has probably been the exemption from capital gains tax on the sale of a main home.

Capital gains tax

During 1988 house prices went up by a massive 25 per cent in real terms. When property markets are booming on this scale, it is tempting to buy and sell, reaping the immediate benefit of the capital investment.

Although "speculative sales" are in theory liable to capital gains tax, it is extremely difficult to prove that profit was the overriding motive for the sale of a person's home. Similarly, home-owners have been trading-up, using the profits from the sale of their existing house to take on a larger mortgage (and a larger property investment).

The exemption from tax on the profit from selling a home is a substantial relief, and had a significant impact on the net wealth of home-owners and on inflating the demand for mortgages during the 1980s.

Mortgage interest tax relief

In 1988 the tax relief on the first £30,000 of a mortgage, at 10.25 per cent interest and at 25p in the £ *standard* income tax, was worth £64 a month. As the interest rates that people were paying on their mortgages subsequently rose to 12 per cent and over, the value rose accordingly.

Around 40 per cent of mortgage interest tax relief goes to taxpayers earning more than £15,000 a year and only 25 per cent to those earning less than £10,000: as a method of targeting relief at those in most need with their housing costs, therefore, the scheme is clearly inequitable. It has meant, however, that many marginal borrowers have been able to buy their own homes.

Until 1988, two people who jointly borrowed to buy a house could *each* claim tax relief on the first £30,000 of the mortgage - in effect raising the ceiling to £60,000. This was a substantial relief, doubling the benefit in the purchase of one property and promoting home ownership among younger age groups and joint, and therefore larger, borrowing. For many young people in the 1980s it was the only way to raise enough money to buy a house.

Double tax relief for all except existing joint mortgages was abolished in the 1988 budget. Also abolished in 1988 was the tax relief on the first £30,000 of a secured loan to finance home improvements. This included replacement loans, or "new for old" improvements, such as house extensions, roof and wall insulation, replacing central heating, even converting a house into flats.

There were few, if any, checks on the use eventually made of such loans and home-owners were able to acquire low-interest credit - that is, a loan with tax relief - without necessarily spending it on home improvements. Home improvement loans were not limited to building societies. So although many borrowers took a further advance on an existing mortgage, many other institutions competed to sell secured lending schemes. How this may have fed into further demand for credit and the development of new credit products is discussed in section 3.2.6.

The result of the lack of verification of the uses actually made of the cash raised through a mortgage has been some "equity leakage" - spending the loan on something other than buying a house or, until 1988, home improvements. People moving house may have taken out larger mortgages than strictly necessary to buy the new property and spent the extra on other goods and services.

The preferential tax status of owner-occupiers is both a cash benefit and a safeguard on the asset value of the property. It may also have inflated consumers' demand for credit and its use for discretionary purposes: we look at whether or not this may constitute a problem in section 3.1.3.

Property tax and housing benefit

"Imputed rent" - the housing services enjoyed by owner-occupiers - has not been taxed since 1963 when schedule A income tax was abolished. Local authority rates represented the last remaining tax on property. These have been replaced by the community charge, in Scotland in 1989 and in England and Wales in 1990. The effect of the abolition of a "property tax" on housing and its related credit markets remains to be seen.

One likely impact of the new community charge is clear. Overall, owner-occupiers will gain, with a shift in the financial burden away from households with large rateable values and/or one adult and towards those with low rateable values and several adults.

Following the 1986 Social Security Act, restrictions were introduced on housing benefit that reduced the number of households eligible for help with their rents and rates. In addition, families on income support who had previously had their rates paid in full became liable to pay 20 per cent of the rates bill. These families are also liable for 20 per cent of the community charge.

The overall effect of the 1986 Act was to tip the balance of advantage between owner-occupiers and tenants further in favour of owner-occupiers.

2.2.3 DEMOGRAPHIC INFLUENCES ON THE DEMAND FOR CREDIT

Birth and death rates, and the relative ages of the population, have a critical effect on credit commitment - an effect often underplayed by commentators. Demographic changes heavily influence the types of credit offered by lenders, and its availability, promotion and marketing. They may also feed into the general level of price competition in the market.

The expenditure patterns of young households, for instance, differ from older ones. Young adults generally buy more consumer durables and use more credit, for different purposes, than older households. See Table II.2 *Credit expenditure on selected items, by age of head of household, 1985.*

In the UK there was an overall rise in the formation of young households in the 1980s, as the baby boom of the early to mid-1960s worked its way through. The crude birth rate peaked at 18.8 births per 1,000 people in 1964. This generation is now reaching its mid-twenties. In 1977 there was a marked fall to 11.7 per 1,000, only slowly climbing to 13.6 per 1,000 ten years later.

The UK has a relatively large proportion of young heads of household compared to the rest of the European Community. New households were forming here at the rate of 175,000 per year during the late 1970s and early 1980s. This swelled the demand for housing, home loans and consumer goods. The growth is forecast to drop back to 110,000 a year during the 1990s.

The numbers of single-person households and households without young children have also increased. In 1976 one in five British households were people living on their own. Ten years later, it was one in four. The rise in the proportion of elderly people, often widowed, is well known. But there has also been a rise in the proportions of people under the age of sixty who live alone, and the number of single-person households is expected to go up further, from 5.2 million in 1986 to a projected 6.6 million by 2001.

In terms of the demand for credit, these are important trends. Credit use declines with age; this may change as a new generation - accustomed to using credit - ages. Furthermore, if the proportion of younger people living on their own has grown, and will grow more, their demand for credit has an effect on overall levels. Demand for other financial services, such as pensions, insurance and home loans, is also affected.

While there has been an absolute increase in the number of young heads of households, there has been a fall in the number with young children. In 1971 18 per cent of households had children under four years old and 21 per cent had children between five and fifteen. Today the proportions are 13 per cent and less than 20 per cent.

Not unexpectedly, families with young children are heavy users of credit. But so are young childless households. The difference between them is why and how they use the money they borrow. Those with children tend to spend it on necessities; those without children appear to use more credit for shorter-term, discretionary spending.

This discretionary element is a complex one to analyse. Some purchases made on credit can be classified as "productive" - cars for business use, for example, and labour-saving items like washing machines. These can be said to represent a form of savings, in that they generate opportunities to earn more. For some households, on the other hand, heavy credit use may represent a form of "dis-saving" - in effect, a weekly or monthly cut in income in order to finance immediate consumption. This is a particularly apt description when the life or value of the purchase dissolves before the end of the credit agreement.

The rise in the number of young childless households means a rise in household budgets freed for purchases of non-necessities - consumer durables, holidays, shares. It also frees the budget for investment in property, and may in turn affect the birth rate, since the decision to borrow heavily to buy a house can mean a young household has to delay starting a family.

In any event, we can expect the trend towards younger household heads and single-person households to be reflected in the whole financial services sector in the last ten years of the century.

Another important, and more widely discussed, trend is our ageing population. This will continue (although at a slower rate than in most of the rest of Europe). In 1987 15.5 per cent of the UK population was over sixty-five years old. By the year 2030, 20 per cent of us will be sixty-five plus.

An ageing population carries with it substantial assets that boost total personal and household wealth. Nearly 93 per cent of owner-occupiers over the age of sixty-five own their property outright. This is 21 per cent of all owner-occupiers.

These properties, unencumbered by mortgage, will be inherited by children likely to be in their mid-forties to early-fifties and who are already home-owners themselves - again of property at or near the end of mortgage terms.

The effect of the inheritance factor on total consumer wealth will be substantial, and is further accelerated by house price rises. Inevitably financial services will be targeted increasingly on an older, more affluent market, and on a generation which - unlike the pre-war generation - is accustomed to the idea of regular and extensive use of credit.

2.3 Consumer access to credit: influences in the 1980s

It is widely assumed that there has been a great change in recent years in people's attitudes towards borrowing money - that they have become casual, even negligent, about overcommitment and debt and that this explains the rise in credit use and indebtedness and default. We examine this assumption in section 2.4.

Here, we look at the other side of the coin: the evidence for a change in attitude on the part of the lenders towards consumers.

The two major trends have been the lenders' approach to young first-time buyers, and their methods of assessing the creditworthiness of applicants.

First-time home buyers

During the 1970s the number of first-time buyers accepted by building societies fell, reaching a low in 1979 of 45 per cent of all home buyers.

This changed in the 1980s, with the proportion of first-time buyers peaking at 53 per cent in 1985, and dropping back to 48 per cent by 1987.

By 1988, one in five of all buyers was under twenty-five years old. Just under two-thirds were under thirty-five.

People buying for the first time tend to borrow more - relative both to their income and to the price of the property - than existing home-owners. Table II.3 *First-time buyers: income, advance and prices* shows the rising ratios of income to advance and advance to price of property between 1979 and 1988.

By 1988, around 25 per cent of first-time buyers had 100 per cent mortgages. Only 5 per cent had loans covering less than half the purchase price. (Almost exactly the reverse applies to loans to existing owner-occupiers.)

For Building Societies Association members alone, in 1986 and 1987 over a half of first-time buyers were granted mortgages of between 95 and 100 per cent of the purchase price. In 1986 more than one in three first-time buyers got advances for 100 per cent or more of the purchase price. (This may have been because of the types of houses being bought - see below.) This dropped to around a quarter in 1988.

In parallel with these figures, the size of the deposits paid by first-time buyers fell during the 1980s. In 1983, 44 per cent put down less than £1,000. In 1986, it was 49 per cent - and nearly one-third paid no deposit at all. More recent figures, however, show lower proportions - with 39 per cent of first-time buyers paying less than £1,000 deposit.

First-time buyers also tend to buy older, smaller property. In 1979, 17 per cent of building society borrowers bought new homes. By 1988 this had fallen to 10 per cent. Sales have also been hit by the decline in public sector housebuilding, which had previously fed through to the sale of council homes. New home completions peaked at 163,000 in 1976 and 1977, falling back to 104,000 in 1979. Since then the decline has continued to 30,000 completions of new public sector homes in 1988. However there has been a revival in the private sector (from 115,000 completions in 1981 to 181,000 by 1988).

This pattern was reversed for pre-1919 homes which rose from 24 per cent of mortgages in 1979 to 28 per cent in 1986, dropping slightly to 27 per cent in 1988. One-third of mortgages were for terraced property and slightly less for semi-detached houses.

In 1979 only 19 per cent of homes being purchased had fewer than five rooms, and 18 per cent had seven or more rooms. By 1988 over one-third had fewer than five rooms and only 11 per cent had more than seven.

So the competitive environment of the 1980s brought about a substantial shift in the policies of lenders towards the younger, less affluent first-time borrower and, following that, towards the overall size and quality of owner-occupied homes. At a time when there was an increase in the supply of credit available from both the retail and wholesale lending markets, mortgagees were forced to lower their lending margins. They took on higher risks - in the borrowers they recruited and on the types of property against which their loans were secured.

There is other evidence for a change in building society lending. Figures from building society surveys are usually adjusted, to reflect the "mix" in the quality of properties being purchased. If first-time buyers are buying lower quality homes, this will be hidden when the figures for house prices are adjusted (4).

A further knock-on effect of the new home buyers' appeal to lenders has been the increase in the demand for additional credit that follows the purchase of older, smaller properties in need of upkeep, renovation, repair and improvement (and in section 1.2.4 we looked at the effect of do-it-yourself on credit demand)

Risk assessment techniques

Developments in credit scoring and credit referencing are examined in detail in section 4. We simply note here the effect that speedier checking of an applicant's creditworthiness has had on access to credit, and on the new customer-oriented, marketing-based policies of the lenders.

There have, then, been major changes in both the policies and practices of the lending institutions towards consumer credit in the past ten years. Has there been an equivalent change in the attitudes of consumers?

2.4 Consumers' attitudes to credit in the 1980s

Ten years ago when we investigated attitudes towards credit (in a survey of 915 people commissioned by the National Consumer Council from the SCPR) views were mixed. Only 6 per cent of people thought it was a "sensible" way of buying goods and services. One in five people thought it was "convenient". There was a general view - held by 43 per cent of respondents - that credit was *occasionally* necessary and a significant minority - just over 25 per cent - who believed that it was *never* a good thing to use credit.

The most recent similar investigation of consumer attitudes was commissioned by the Office of Fair Trading in 1987. This - the *Consumers' Use of Credit Survey* - seems to indicate that, while credit use was escalating, people's attitudes to it were still a mixture of pro and con. Table II.4 *Consumer attitudes to credit 1987* gives the list of statements about credit with which respondents were asked to agree or disagree.

The strongest agreement seems to focus around the potential dangers of borrowing money, and the importance of living within one's means. The statement *On the whole credit is a good thing* received, interestingly for 1987, a tepid response. Fifty-eight per cent agreed with it, but only 13 per cent agreed strongly. Those aged between twenty-five and forty-four, and from the higher social and income brackets, gave the more positive responses.

It is clear from the 1987 survey that people are conscious of the hazards of credit commitment and of the need for control to be exercised by lenders as well as by individual consumers. A formidable 92 per cent agreed (strongly or slightly) that the amount lent should be linked to the borrower's earnings and 69 per cent that there should be tighter regulation of advertisements for credit - both views emphasising the responsibilities of the lenders. Eighty-four per cent agreed that credit limits should be increased only at the request of the customer and 90 per cent that *people don't think enough before taking out credit* - attitudes that acknowledge the borrower's responsibilities.

The reasons consumers give for using credit show some interesting shifts between the 1979 and 1987 surveys. In 1979 only 20 per cent agreed that credit was "a convenient way of buying". Eight years later, "convenience" was selected (from a series of statements) as the most important factor by 52 per cent of credit users (who were 63 per cent of the sample).

In 1987, however, "necessity" also rated highly among credit users.

There were significant variations in the reasons for using credit among different income, age and social groups, and by work status. See Table II.5 *Reasons for using credit, by age, social class and presence of children in the household* and Table II.6 *Reasons for using credit, by personal income and employment status 1987.*

At one end of the spectrum, older people and those with higher incomes and in a higher social class see credit as a *convenient* way of buying goods and services. At the other, the younger, less well-off and lower socioeconomic groups see credit as a means of paying for things that they *need* and could not otherwise afford.

Different sorts of borrowers have always used different sorts of credit, in different ways. The gentry "ran up bills"; the pauper pawned her wedding ring. But credit of most kinds was seen as a standby, to be used when you were in need rather than for the sake of convenience, and certainly most debt was traditionally frowned upon. This seems to have changed.

Credit is no longer viewed exclusively as an emergency measure, to be used for the necessities of life. For many people, it is becoming a way of acquiring discretionary goods, to underwrite immediate consumption.

This is important, and might be taken to confirm a widespread feeling that people are no longer prepared to wait and save before they satisfy the wish to acquire luxury items. But it may also imply - especially given the ages and incomes of those who view credit, above all, as a convenience - that the level of personal wealth is now such that most borrowers could, if required to, afford to pay for these goods and services; they postpone payment because it is handy to do so. The corollary of this will be that credit is being used less by the poorer consumer (in terms of net income) than by the better-off. We look at the evidence for and against this hypothesis in section 3.3.1.

2.5 Proxy credit: electricity, gas, water and rent commitments

Most people do not count their electricity or the rent as a means of borrowing. But in practice, for the majority who pay their bills in arrears, that is precisely what they are. And deferred payment can mount into a heavy commitment, which may feed into demand for yet further credit.

Nearly every household sometimes delays paying the fuel, water or rent bills in order to meet other family expenditure. It provides a form of interest-free loan and has been identified (5) as one common way of stretching a heavily committed household budget. For a family in temporary financial straits, deferred settlement of one or two of these bills may be a successful strategy.

However, for a minority, it brings catastrophe. As a source of loan, it is strictly limited in time, and can lead to multiple debts and - in the case of fuel, power or water supplies - to disconnection from an essential lifeline service. Research by the Policy Studies Institute has shown a disproportionate number of unemployed people among gas and electricity debtors and those subsequently disconnected (5).

By a curious anomaly, the electricity and gas boards do not have to obtain a court order before cutting a customer off from their services for non-payment. All that is necessary is a magistrate's warrant if the supplier needs to enter premises. This distinguishes the fuel boards from other creditors. In effect, where there are multiple debts, they are preferential creditors. Here we look at the available figures for fuel and water disconnections and for rent arrears as a measure of these forms of credit.

Electricity and gas commitments

Around 22 million people are consumers of electricity. More than 78,500 of them were disconnected for non-payment of their electricity bills in England and Wales in 1988/89.

This is a high figure but in fact was lower than for any other year in the decade. The trend for disconnections has been falling since the early 1980s - over 118,000 were disconnected in 1980/81 - probably as a result of revisions to the industry's voluntary code of practice. A sudden rise in 1985/86 proved temporary, partly reflecting a rise in charges the year before and partly perhaps the lagged effect of economic recession. See Table II.7 *Electricity disconnections for non-payment, England and Wales.*

There were wide variations between individual area boards both in the numbers of homes disconnected and in the number that remained disconnected.

But while the disconnections rate is a useful indicator of financial difficulties, and particularly of overcommitment on "proxy credit", it is only part of the picture. Pre-payment or token meters, "fuel direct" deductions from welfare benefits, and the rate of referrals to advice and other agencies by the fuel boards all point to a rise in fuel poverty over the period.

The numbers of consumers who made repayment arrangements (including prepayment meters) or "fuel direct" payments through welfare benefit rose from around 140,000 in 1984 to 163,000 in 1986. In a 1986 paper, Gillian Parker made an educated guess at 1.5 million electricity consumers in difficulty with repayment (6). This is 7.5 per cent of all domestic consumers. The level may now have increased slightly.

There are around 16 million domestic gas consumers. In 1988 the Gas Consumers Council published a detailed analysis of gas disconnections (7) which is only briefly summarised here.

Between 1979 and 1988 households were disconnected by the gas board when they were, on average, seven months in arrears. As with electricity, there were regional variations in disconnection rates for gas. This is attributed to different interpretations of the voluntary code of practice (8) and different management practices, rather than the susceptibility of some parts of the country to get into debt.

Table II.8 shows the level of gas disconnections for non-payment from 1979 to 1988, a rise from a base of 100 in 1979 to 137 in 1988. There was a sudden very sharp rise in 1987 (when it went to 170), attributed to the fewer prepayment coin meters installed by the boards for their customers early that year. A new agreement with British Gas, to offer consumers a meter as an alternative to disconnection, was announced in January 1989. However, there apparently remained some differences between the regional gas boards as to when they would supply meters. The gas industry's code of practice is now a provision of the privatised industry's licence.

Between 1983 and 1987 the average debt on disconnection was £200, varying between £255 for the northern region to a low of £156 for north-eastern region consumers.

As we have mentioned, other creditors have to pursue sums like this through the county courts where, overall, two out of three money plaints are for less than £500. The National Consumer Council has consistently urged an end to the privileged status of the public utilities which are able to use their monopoly power to collect past debts by threatening disconnection of an essential service. We discussed the anomaly most recently in our report on legal services and the courts in England and Wales, *Ordinary Justice* (9) and recommended that if the right to disconnect for past debts is retained at all, it should only be permitted by express order in the county court.

The privatisation of the gas industry brought a new obligation to British Gas - to apply for a licence governing their showroom credit sales. We trust that a similar provision will apply to the privatised electricity industry. At the time of writing, before the proposed sale of the electricity supply companies, electricity board showrooms do not require a licence to sell, for instance, ovens or central heating on credit terms. The board may offer, or indeed demand, that any arrears on these credit purchases are added to the customer's electricity bill. This can suddenly overload a previously up-to-date quarterly fuel bill and in many cases push the consumer into default and then disconnection.

Water rates commitments

Domestic disconnections for arrears of water rates have been increasing
since 1984 (when the figures were published for the first time).

Table II.9 gives the available number and level of household disconnections from 1984/85 to 1988/89. These figures are certainly less than the
total. They cover England only, and they exclude disconnections by the
statutory water companies which serve around a quarter of all consumers.
However, they are included to give a general picture.

Since the average household bill for water rates in England and Wales
in 1986/87 was £97.18, we can assume that consumers were disconnected
for owing relatively small sums of money.

The legislation providing for the sale of the water industry in 1990 gave
consumer organisations the opportunity to lobby for change, especially on
the systems covering disconnection for non-payment. Under the Water Act
1989, the procedures for disconnecting consumers from their water supply
are laid down in the licensing provisions. Essentially, debtors are now
protected from disconnection if they comply with a court judgement to
repay what they owe at a given rate. If they fail to abide by the judgement,
or if another court order for further repayments is taken out by the creditor,
disconnection may follow. So unlike the electricity and gas suppliers, water
boards must go through the courts for repayment. Any breaches of the
detailed disconnection procedure will be dealt with under the statutory
licensing provisions. (See (10) for a full discussion.)

"Credit" through rent arrears

Rent payments are another form of proxy credit, fully described by Ungerson
and Baldock in their 1978 study of rent arrears in Ashford (11) and in a
similar study by Kirby and Duncan (12). In practice, as with fuel and
water debts, serious rent arrears may have only a tenuous connection with
other credit use. The problem behind rent arrears is often the consumer's
basic inadequacy of income. It is important to bear this in mind when
considering the extent to which 'real' consumer credit precipitates debt
problems.

Full statistics on rent arrears in both the public and private sectors are
sporadic. The Audit Commission published one of the largest studies of
council tenant rent arrears in 1984 (13). A recent repeat survey (14) indicates
that during 1988 these arrears rose from £100 million to £450 million. The
annual figures published by the Chartered Institute of Public Finance and
Accountancy are for England and Wales only and include rates and heating
charges, plus any arrears of previous tenants. They are based on local
authority returns. In addition, arrears are calculated from week one up,
unlike the figures for mortgages. So there are elements of both under- and
over-estimates in these figures.

Table II.10 shows local authority rent arrears for England and Wales,
rising from 3 per cent of total collectable rent in 1977 to 5.8 per cent in
1986. In 1986 this represented over £200 million.

The problem is more acute in inner city and metropolitan areas where it is estimated that almost half of the accounts were in default in 1984 (12). In London, public sector rent arrears rose by 24 per cent in 1987/88, from £84 million to £104 million. Housing association rent arrears also rose (15).

Earlier researchers commented on the importance of the benefits system in cutting the level of rent arrears. This seems to have reversed, with the reforms of social security and housing benefit introduced in April 1988 and the requirement that claimants pay 20 per cent of their rates/community charge. A survey of four London housing associations (16), carried out three months after April 1988, showed a worrying 25 per cent increase in arrears: the researchers estimated that total arrears exceeded £1.9 million - £1 million of which was over and above any underlying trend.

SUMMARY: DEBT AND PROXY CREDIT

The levels of total outstanding commitment on electricity, gas, water and rent gives us a picture - although a simplistic one - of the networks of borrowing used by consumers in financial difficulty. The root of the problem may be poor housekeeping and wilful overcommitment. More commonly, according to research, the reason is inadequate income for the bare essentials or a sudden crisis such as sickness, redundancy or bereavement.

The difference is important. The overall levels of debt include these multiple commitments and without detailed studies, it is virtually impossible to isolate the use, or misuse, of credit as the single catalyst of insolvency. More influential are the networks of borrowing, the responses of different creditors and the latitude available to the borrower to cut their standard of living. This has been discussed by various researchers (17 and 18). They stress the need to examine default as the result of a whole set of factors, often interrelated. Simply to attribute serious money problems to "illness", "bereavement" or "unemployment" ignores the critical question of why some people become seriously overindebted while others, in seemingly identical circumstances, manage. This has implications in our search for solutions to the problems of indebtedness and overcommitment, discussed further in section 5.

2.6 Legal action against consumer debtors

We have seen the numbers of people using fuel and other commitments as a source of credit. These consumers are approaching the far end of the manageable/unmanageable credit spectrum. Here we look briefly at those who have travelled even further towards insolvency, with the figures for legal actions against non-payers. However, it must be remembered that these give no unequivocal clues about the origins of financial problems that end up in court; overcommitment may not be the whole story.

The *Judicial Statistics* (19) from which we take our figures are for England and Wales only. They may contain other trends than a rise or fall in personal financial difficulties: creditors sometimes alter their policies, for instance, and decide to pursue arrears more vigorously by taking more debtors to court. Indeed, banks and finance houses took out four times more actions against defaulters in the county courts in 1987 than in 1980 and accounted for 11.2 per cent of all money plaints in 1987 compared with 3.7 per cent in 1979. And some creditors are more litigious than others: around half the claims issued in 1987 were brought by just fifty creditors (20). The *Statistics* also contain an unidentified proportion of business debts.

Many studies have shown that court actions and seizure of goods for debt are most often for relatively small sums of money and for non-luxury goods. Recent figures (19) show that a quarter of all money plaints in the county courts were for less than £100 and almost two in three were for less than £500. These are similar to the findings of the Touche Ross study for the Civil Justice Review (21): 75 per cent of claims in their county court study were for sums of less than £500. However, 11 per cent were for larger sums - £1,000 to £2,000. While overall the debts taken to court seem quantitatively small, individual creditors vary markedly in the amounts they choose to pursue.

Ninety per cent of the 2,375,431 recovery plaints entered in the county courts in 1987 were claims for money; the rest were for recovery of land and "miscellaneous". The steep climb in actions to recover both money and land in the ten years is striking. Actions for land and residential premises went up by 50 per cent after 1979. In section 3.2.5 we examine the background to a rising trend in mortgage arrears and repossession.

Clues about the categories of creditor taking action through the courts are thin. We have already mentioned the increase in claims from the "traditional" lenders - banks and finance houses, and moneylenders - which now account for 13 per cent of claims (and for larger amounts than other creditors). See Table II.11. *The nature and size of plaints in the county courts, 1987.*

Attachment of earnings orders - to enforce payment of a judgement debt - also increased, peaking at well over 64,000 in 1985, and dropping back to just over 53,000 in 1987. See Table II.12. *Attachment of earnings, applications and orders, 1980-1987.*

The *Judicial Statistics* do not identify other types of creditor. Nonetheless, other research has shown that the public utilities (gas, electricity, phones and water) are the biggest *users* of the courts for debt recovery, with thousands of summonses each month (21). A high proportion of the actions brought in the county courts may therefore involve debts owed to public utilities and local authorities. As we have said already, these figures are less useful as a means of investigating default in commercial credit transactions, but they are sound indicators of overall domestic money difficulties.

References to section 2

1. Scottish Special Housing Association, *Clearing the Fog: the social security reforms in focus*, Market Research Scotland, 1989.
2. David Fetcher, "Millions are aided by safety net for poor", *Daily Telegraph*, 21/7/89, p.16.
3. "Budget pressures threaten benefits", *Observer*, 30/7/89, p.8.
4. Patrick Foley, 'House price boom or bust', *Lloyds Bank Economic Bulletin*, no. 93, September 1986.
5. Richard Berthoud, *Fuel Debts and Hardship*, report no. 601, Policy Studies Institute, 1981.
6. Gillian Parker, "Consumers in debt", paper given to the *Consumers in Debt* conference organised by the National Consumer Council, 1986.
7. Gas Consumers Council, *An Analysis of Gas Disconnections*, GCC, February 1988.
8. Gas Consumers Council, *Fuel Debts and Hardship: the working of the revised code of practice*, GCC, 1985.
9. National Consumer Council, *Ordinary Justice: legal services and the courts in England and Wales*, HMSO, 1989.
10. Debate on the Water Bill in the House of Lords, *Hansard*, 18 May 1989, col. 1299-1300.
11. Clare Ungerson and John Baldock, *Rent Arrears in Ashford*, Department of Social Administration and Social Work, University of Kent, Canterbury, 1978.
12. S. Duncan and K. Kirby, *Preventing Rent Arrears*, HMSO, 1983.
13. Audit Commission, *Bringing Council Tenants' Arrears Under Control*, HMSO, 1984.
14. Audit Commission, *Survey of Local Authority Housing Rent Arrears*, HMSO, 1989.
15. Janet Ford, *The Indebted Society: credit and default in the 1980s*, Routledge, 1988.
16. CES Ltd, *The Social Security Act and Rent Arrears in Housing Associations*, research report no. 3, National Federation of Housing Associations, 1989.
17. J. Doling and others, *A Property Owning Democracy*, Gower, 1988.
18. Pauline Ashley, *The Money Problems of the Poor: a literature review*, Heinemann, 1983. (SSRC/DHSS studies in deprivation and disadvantage, no. II.)
19. Lord Chancellor's Department, *Judicial Statistics England and Wales, for the Year 1987*, HMSO, 1988, Cm 428.
20. Michael Kron, "Default procedures", a paper given at the *Cards on the Table* conference sponsored by Lovell White Durrant and the Money Management Council, June 1988.
21. Touche Ross Management Consultants, *Study of Debt Enforcement Procedures*, carried out for the Civil Justice Review, Lord Chancellor's Department, December 1986.

3. Credit and consumer concerns

In this section we explore the impact of the surge in personal borrowing on particular categories of consumer, and identify some of the problems, often in terms of repayment and credit use.

We look at: home owners, and particularly first-time buyers and other marginal home loan borrowers; and then at other borrowers vulnerable to credit overcommitment - families with children, young adults, students, unemployed people, low-income families and the elderly. We also discuss two specific credit products that raise some concerns - credit cards (already widely popular) and equity lending (likely to become so); and finally look at how consumers make their decisions about credit, and the information on which they base those decisions.

Our review is concerned with the consumer perspective on credit, and on whether the market provides consumers with sufficient, and efficient, access, choice, information, equity, value for money and redress. We are conscious, of course, that there is much concern about the wider economic effects of a high level of credit demand, and its potential to feed into inflation. While this is an important issue, it is beyond the scope of this review of the *consumer* issues, and we only refer to the wider economic arguments in passing.

Much of our evidence in this section draws on three surveys commissioned by the Office of Fair Trading and on the OFT's subsequent report. We refer to that report, and to the three surveys on which it was based, using the shorthand phrases:

OFT (1989) for *Overindebtedness*, a report by the Director General of Fair Trading, May 1989

PAS (1987) for *Consumers' Use of Credit Survey* by PAS Business Surveys for the Office of Fair Trading, 1987

PAS (1989) for *Omnibus Survey* by PAS Business Surveys for the Office of Fair Trading, 1989

FES (1986) for *Reanalysis of the Family Expenditure Survey, 1986 data*, Office of Fair Trading, 1989

There is no dispute about the fact that the amount of outstanding consumer credit increased during the 1980s. But in a recent discussion, Ford (1) raised the question: has there been a rise in the absolute numbers of people who borrow, or is it that existing credit users are borrowing more?

The OFT (1989) research suggests that, while both are likely to be true, the growth in the number of borrowers is far lower than the growth in the amount of repayments. The PAS (1987) survey, for instance, provides evidence for the longstanding impression that credit commitment rises as a person's income rises, only tailing off at incomes over £20,000 a year. (Ford plots this as a rising S-shaped curve.) And the FES (1986) data confirms that repayments on mortgages and credit commitments rise with income, in a steep curve.

People are more heavily committed than they were. But the higher income groups are borrowing larger sums more often and from a widening range of sources. As a result, the level of repayments is rising proportionately more than the total number of credit users. This may mask the true extent of repayment difficulties among those on low and middle incomes.

The OFT (1989) report also highlights the relatively large increase in the numbers of both mortgaged and non-mortgaged borrowers with other credit commitments in the short period between the 1987 and the 1989 surveys.

	PAS 1987	PAS 1987 adjusted	PAS 1989
% of those with mortgages who also have commitments	67	56	73
% of those with no mortgage who have credit commitments	40	30	42
% of those with credit commitments who also have mortgages	51	53	60

Source: OFT/PAS 1989.

This may be explained partly by the announcement in spring 1988 of the end of double tax relief on joint mortgages and the subsequent rush to buy before the deadline in the autumn. The same budget also gave taxpayers a windfall that may have affected consumer spending and encouraged people to take on more credit.

We now turn to the effects of wider credit commitment on particular groups of consumers.

3.1 Home owners

As we have seen (section 1), mortgage lending was a major growth area of the 1980s. Nearly three-quarters of the mortgages on building society books in 1989 were taken out after 1981; it is reasonable to assume that the bulk of home loans from other institutions are equally recent.

The competition for new customers in the 1980s pushed lenders 'down-market'. Demographic factors (the 'baby boomers') and the reduction in numbers of homes for rent have also played their part. The UK has more young home owners than most countries in the European Community. This may have precipitated a variety of problems.

Young home owners tend to take on financial commitments while their income is rising. At the same time, though, they are acquiring personal commitments - partners, spouses, children - that expand their financial needs. And their need is likely to be highest at precisely the time when joint incomes fall, through pregnancy and parenthood. The loss of one of two incomes contributing to a joint mortgage can stretch budgets paper thin, creating even greater reliance on credit.

The problem is compounded for new home owners who are 'marginal' borrowers (in terms of disposable income) or whose work is subject to seasonal fluctuations.

Of course the picture is a familiar one to a great many people at some time in their lives. Most muddle through - cutting back on luxuries, turning to mum and dad. These have always been economic facts of family life.

But what may be new is the *scale* of the problem - the number of 'failures' in the housing market and the higher social and economic costs for the individuals who are affected and for society at large. Statistics in support of this view are not readily available, but we offer some indicators.

3.1.1 MORTGAGE ARREARS AND REPOSSESSIONS

The statistics on repossession of homes, like others relating to credit commitment and insolvency, are not completely straightforward. Some homes, for instance, are surrendered voluntarily for reasons not necessarily to do with the household finances. Some lenders publish their figures (notably the Building Societies Association and the Council of Mortgage Lenders), while others do not. Most of the available figures refer to arrears of six months and over, so that shorter-term repayment difficulties are not reported. And they refer to possessions as a proportion of all current loans.

The figures that are available show that repossessions increased sharply in 1980-87, fell back in 1988, and rose sharply again in late 1989. It is likely that overall house price figures were artificially depressed in 1979-81 with the sales of local authority homes to sitting tenants at reduced prices, and very recent figures came at a time when the mortgage market was 'under-lent', following the rise in interest rates in autumn 1988. It might be useful, therefore, to look at trends in repossessions over a longer time period than for most of the data in this book.

Table III.1 shows *the percentage changes in building society repossessions, and house prices, 1970-88.* There appears to be an inverse relationship between house prices and repossession rates. When prices are falling, or static, the number of homes repossessed rises. When prices go up, repossessions fall.

This is the logical response for people facing repayment difficulties, of course. When prices are rising it is sensible to hold on to your major asset, even if this is a struggle. When prices are falling, with the chance that they may drop further, it makes more sense to cut your losses.

This has implications for the early 1990s. During 1989 house prices were stable and even fell, particularly in the south east. (Households in the south east are also likely to be the most heavily committed in terms of mortgage repayments and other credit.) Interest rates on mortgages stayed high. If the housing market continues to fall, many more owner-occupiers struggling to make ends meet may decide to surrender their homes before the situation gets any worse. Alternatively, they may come to rely more and more on other credit to keep afloat, with serious implications for households already heavily committed.

A proportion of home-owners in financial difficulties will also take the opportunity to trade down, buying a less expensive property. Unfortunately, during the latter half of 1989 falling house prices were accompanied by high and rising interest rates and comparatively low inflation. Instead of being able to sell a property and repay the mortgage - as in the early 1970s when high interest rates were partnered by rising prices - home owners trying to sell were (as we went to press) making a loss. This has important implications, as the emerging figures on arrears show.

While formal statistics were not yet available as we were writing this, there had been reports of increased mortgage arrears. The Woolwich Building Society, for example, was reported (in the *Independent*, 11 November 1989) as comparing the 1988 figure of 5 per cent of accounts three months in arrears with a new figure of 7.5 per cent for the first three quarters of 1989. Ford (in unpublished research) has also noted a 23 per cent rise in mortgages two months in arrears, between December 1988 and July 1989. The Building Societies Association figures for December 1988 and June 1989, on accounts between six and twelve months in arrears, also show a 20 per cent increase. In addition, homes surrendered voluntarily rose from a third of all repossessions in early 1989 to 43 per cent by the end of the year.

New lending by building societies continued in 1989 but much more slowly than in 1988. Net new lending in the first three months of 1989 was 33 per cent down on the previous year. This leaves extra funds with lenders, enabling them to absorb a higher level of arrears. And indeed it is not in their interests to repossess when house prices are falling.

Table III.1 shows the percentage changes in repossessions. It does not show the absolute rise in the number of households giving up their homes. As we have seen, the number of mortgages held increased rapidly during the 1980s - from 5.3 million in 1979 to 7.5 million in 1988. This was a 42 per cent increase. However, repossessions stood at 2,530 a year in 1979, peaked at nearly 23,000 during 1987, and fell back in 1988. This represented a rise of over 800 per cent - far greater than the increase in mortgages held.

This leads us to the figures for arrears as distinct from repossessions. See Table III.2 *Building society arrears, 1979-88*. Again, the statistics have to be used cautiously. The proportion of loans in arrears shows a clear upward trend to 1985, fluctuating slightly after that. A peak year for arrears was 1985, when nearly 50,000 households were six to twelve months behind with their mortgage repayments. In fact in the six years after 1979, these arrears had grown at a rate eighteen times faster than the number of outstanding loans.

In 1987 over 61,000 loans were in arrears of more than six months. This fell by about a quarter in 1988. However, the mortgage rate rise in late-1988 may have affected this fall. Certainly the numbers of those in arrears of more than six months on their mortgage increased - from 46,370 in 1988 to 54,360 in the first half of 1989. The increase was more substantial for loans between six and twelve months in arrears. We examine the combined effect of interest rate rises and income tax reductions in section 3.1.2 below.

In 1988 first-time buyers borrowed an average £30,374 from building societies - ranging from a high of £53,729 in Greater London to a low of £18,934 in Scotland (2). On an advance of £30,000, the initial repayment in mid-1988 would have been around £239 per month. By January 1989 this had gone up to £297 per month - an increase of almost 25 per cent.

So from January 1989 a household in 'serious' arrears (counted by the industry as six months or more) was faced with an outstanding commitment of at least £1,800, plus the ongoing monthly repayments of £297. Even three months arrears would have meant nearly £1,000 owing. Especially for the first-time buyer - whose average income in 1988 was £14,103 - the rise would have stretched the household budget towards breaking point. One researcher estimates that mortgage holders needed an increase in income of about 14 per cent to cope with the repayment increases, or 20 per cent for people who had recently moved house (3).

3.1.2 WHICH HOUSEHOLDS ARE MOST AT RISK?

It is worth trying to identify those home buyers and owners most at risk of credit overcommitment.

The PAS (1987 and 1989) surveys did not distinguish between new and existing home owners. They did, however, distinguish between housing tenures - rented, owned outright, owned on a mortgage, and others. The analysis of the FES (1986) data is revealing. See Table III.3 *Credit (excluding mortgage) repayments, by households with different housing tenures, 1986.*

Overall, nearly 37 per cent of householders had non-mortgage credit commitments, representing weekly repayments of an average £18.30. But for people with a mortgage, this rose to 57 per cent with other credit commitments, repaying an average £21 a week.

Of course, not everyone buying their home is at risk of overcommitment. Even level of income is not a reliable guide: pensioners, with among the lowest household incomes, are the least likely to be overcommitted. The crucial element is the relationship between income and repayment obligations. See Table III.4 *Weekly credit and mortgage commitments of those buying their homes, by income, 1986.*

Not surprisingly we find that weekly commitments vary with income. In 1986 households with a weekly income of around £90 were committed to weekly credit payments of around £23.30. At the other end of the scale, households with a weekly income of £500-plus had weekly repayments of £48.40. Clearly the important features are the absolute amounts owed each week and the proportion of income this represents.

A weekly repayment of £23 deducted from an income of £90 leaves very little, for instance, for large quarterly electricity or gas bills. The OFT (1989) report identifies those most at financial risk as households with a weekly income between £100 and £175 per week: this was a little below the mean weekly wage for 1989.

Just over a quarter of first-time buyers with a building society mortgage had incomes below £9,000 in 1988. Their repayments, already high in relation to income, were slightly eased by the income tax benefits of the 1988 budget, only to be pushed up again by the interest rates.

A first-time buyer on £9,000 a year will typically be granted a mortgage of around £20,000 - just over the average 2.15 times annual income. This is how the income and mortgage repayments would have worked out between January and October 1988:

Mortgage	*Income*
£20,000	£9,000

January 1988: interest rate 10.3% (7.5% net)
Monthly income

after tax	£556.87
mortgage repayment	149.77
net income	407.10

October 1988: interest rate 12.75% (9.56% net)
Monthly income

after tax	£571.80
mortgage repayment	
net income	177.47
	394.33

So the weekly mortgage for this less well-off home buyer rose to around £44 a week - even before the February 1990 rate rise.

In the early 1980s, 'right to buy' households were over-represented among those on low incomes wanting to buy a house. As competition increased among lenders and they began to recruit lower-income borrowers, the emphasis on local authority home buyers lessened. Nonetheless, local authority homes - many in the first three to five years of mortgage repayments - feature proportionately highly among repossessions. See Table

III.5 *Local authority and building society mortgage repossessions and arrears, England, 1980-88.*

A significant and growing proportion of council house waiting list clients are owner-occupiers (22 per cent in non-metropolitan areas in 1987 (4)). And the number of cases where homelessness is due mainly to mortgage default and whom local authorities agree to rehouse has also been rising steadily. (See Table III.6 *Households accepted for rehousing by local authorities where main reason is mortgage default or arrears, England and Wales, 1979-88.*) In 1988 this was 10 per cent of rehoused families. In some regions the percentage is higher. In East Hertfordshire District Council mortgage default accounted for 6 per cent of rehousing acceptances in 1982, rising to 22 per·cent in 1987. A similar leap was recorded for Tendring District Council (5)

A Department of the Environment study on homeless people (6) reported that the most common reason for becoming homeless (mentioned by 23 per cent of the sample) was connected with marriage breakdown. There was a specific reference to mortgage arrears by 10 per cent in the south of England. The researchers point out that this is significant, bearing in mind that DoE statistics show that 80 per cent of the households in temporary accommodation in 1987 lived in the south east and London.

Unemployment, according to most lenders, has not been a major factor in mortgage arrears. This may be because redundancy payments are used to settle outstanding debts, including mortgages, or because unemployment is concentrated among tenants rather than owner-occupiers. However, the loss of a job can hit individual mortgage holders hard, particularly if it happens in the early years of a loan when repayments may account for as much as 25 per cent of monthly income.

Entitlement to social security benefit may have offset the most pressing financial worries. Interest payments on mortgages to owner-occupiers had already been cut prior to 1988. It remains to be seen whether the further changes in the benefits system in 1988 lead to more repossessions.

3.1.3 CREDIT COMMITMENT: INVESTMENT OR CONSUMPTION?

Are consumers employing their vastly increased use of credit to invest in assets that will appreciate, or to finance instant consumption? By taking together the figures for income and expenditure and for debt and wealth, we can produce a broad estimate of how assets and liabilities are balanced.

A London Business School calculation indicates that while the debt:income ratio rose steeply from 1979/80, the debt:wealth ratio remained remarkably steady - largely because of the increase in the population's investment assets (although there was a drop in 1987 following the October stock market crash) (7). See Table III.7 *Personal sector debt:income and debt:wealth ratios, 1971-1987/88.*

Home loans and other types of credit, as we have seen, rose substantially in the 1980s. But if borrowers are taking on the further commitments to finance home improvements and repairs, for instance, they are clearly investing in the future value of their property. In theory, there is less cause for concern if those who are borrowing heavily are also those who have an investment income or an appreciating asset.

There are certainly more shareholders than there were, rising from 7 per cent of the population in 1979 to just over 20 per cent in 1988. Some of this sharebuying will have been financed through loans and revolving credit.

However, unearned *income* from shares and dividends, and from property, only contributes significantly to households in the top-income groups. Unearned income in the lower and middle-income groups comes predominantly from building society accounts (accounting for 60 per cent of the unearned income of the lowest-income earners). See Table III.8 *Investment income, by type of investment and household income, 1986.*

So net wealth remains closely related to original income and the rise in the number of shareholders is unlikely to have made a substantial impact on the net income of lower earners.

Reliable data on the link between asset-holding and credit commitment are rare. But building society figures, for instance, do imply that their investors are not the same people as their borrowers. See Table III.9 *Age distribution of mortgage-holding investors and borrowers, 1989.*

The OFT (1989) report on credit use also looked at net wealth, asset-holding and credit commitment. See Table III.10 *Relationship between credit commitment and income, 1987* and Table III.11 *Relationship between personal/ joint credit commitments and selected assets, 1987.* These show that the more you earn, the more likely you are to use credit, and to owe more.

The lowest (nil owing) and highest (owing more than £5,000) credit commitment categories included more respondents who held stocks and shares, property assets and savings certificates than other categories. There may be an age-related effect, since those owning their homes outright (53 per cent of whom were aged over sixty-five) made up a third of the lower group and it is known that pensioners are generally very low users of credit.

The heavy credit users (those owing more than £5,000 exclusive of a first mortgage) are largely represented by thirty-five to forty-four year olds - three times as many have commitments in this category as those aged sixty-five plus or twenty-five to thirty-four. They were also overwhelmingly buying their home on a mortgage (97 per cent). While it is important to note the appreciating value of property, there has been a regional disparity in property values that has only recently begun to stabilise.

Overall, it is probable that the rise in credit, of which mortgage debt is the largest slice, has been matched by a rise in liquid (e.g. shares) and frozen (e.g. property) assets. Certainly the value of any property rose substantially (and more in the south east than elsewhere) during the 1980s. Home owners have become asset-rich. One analyst estimates that between 1985 and 1987 house prices accounted for about 60 per cent of the increase in net wealth (8).

However, we have also seen some home owners become asset-rich but cash-poor. Traditionally, the home loans market represented a fairly homogeneous, 'affluent' credit sector. This is changing. Studies on default (9) and the OFT (1989) survey indicate the emergence of a group of marginal, lower-income, high-credit borrowers. They tend to be young, with children, self-employed or 'intermittently wealthy'.

It is very likely that during the 1980s, new mortgage borrowers increased their credit commitments at a rate disproportionate to the equity they could in practice command at any one time. The cash-poor may also have cashed in part of their assets, both for necessities, like urgent house repairs, and for discretionary goods and services.

Given the trend towards longer-term secured lending, we can assume a small but growing pool of home loan consumers who are at very high risk of financial overcommitment.

Over 80 per cent of credit is secured against property. The quality of the credit industry's debt is intimately related to the value of that property. We can expect changes in net income and changes in property prices to have serious repercussions.

The 1989 down-turn in house prices, notably in south east England, was accompanied by sharp rises in interest rates. No changes in these trends had been signalled at the time of writing. For households on the financial margins, there has been severe strain, spilling into arrears. A spate of house sales, forced on families facing serious overcommitment or enforced by creditors, would further depress house prices, and consequently the quality of the debts secured on those houses. In these circumstances, lenders may find their ratio of risk to return rising unacceptably high.

3.2 Other vulnerable borrowers

The Office of Fair Trading (1989) report makes some national estimates of the numbers of consumers at risk - actually or potentially - of overcommitment:

★ around 2 million people have 'heavy' credit commitments;
★ around 3.5 million people feel that their commitments are too high;
★ around 8 million people have taken on commitments they later regretted;
★ it could be expected that around 4.5 million people experienced difficulties with repayments over the previous five years;
★ a quarter of those with difficulties are likely to have had them as a result of unemployment.

Some of these borrowers will be the new and existing mortgage holders discussed in section 3.1 above. But not all of them. In this section we look at the other categories of people at most risk of running into trouble with credit commitments.

A combined picture of the at-risk groups is drawn in the PAS (1987) survey. See Tables III.12 *Profile of those thinking their current commitments are too high*, Table III.13 *Profile of those taking on commitments they had later regretted* and Table III.14 *Profile of those having difficulty in keeping up credit repayments in the past five years*.

These are subjective assessments of individual credit commitments, but they bear out the more detailed findings of the OFT's surveys and endorse other earlier evidence about the people likely to encounter repayment problems (10, 11 and 12).

3.2.1 HOUSEHOLDS WITH CHILDREN

According to the PAS (1987) survey, while a third of the households in the total sample included children under sixteen, over half of the at-risk households had children under sixteen. This bears out a number of earlier surveys. Gregory and Monk, for example, found that compared to the population as a whole, families in debt were larger, with three or more dependent children, and included fewer small households (13).

Indebtedness is therefore closely related to the family life cycle. Early married life may initially be relatively affluent, especially if both partners are working, and credit may be used more often for discretionary spending (although the 1980s trend towards house purchase by more lower-income couples is likely to have affected this). The birth of a child brings greater dependency on a single income, at least for a period. With more children, the pressure on income increases and credit is used more for necessities than luxuries.

Many families weather this period of financial strain and gradually get more control over their budgeting. But the evidence from studies of people going for money advice and debt counselling indicate that the number of households with debt problems is increasing, that the problems are more severe, and that they are lasting longer (11 and 14).

The figures for 'non-consumer credit', such as public utility debts, cannot be separated out. But it is likely that commitments for electricity, gas, water and so on feature high in the budget stretch of families with children.

As for consumer credit, repayment difficulties occur most often with credit cards (25 per cent), followed by bank and building society loans (20 per cent) and mortgages (18 per cent). A change in employment status was given as the major precipitating factor for repayment difficulties among households with children.

3.2.2 YOUNGER BORROWERS

The PAS (1987) survey examined the attitudes of sixteen to seventeen year olds. Although having a good awareness of credit sources, they were vague on the relative costs and merits of each type. Experience of credit was almost exclusively limited to mail order but only 1 per cent said that they did not expect to use credit by the time they were twenty-five years old. We can expect demand to remain high as these youngsters get older.

Of those aged eighteen to twenty-four, over 20 per cent said that they had had difficulties with credit repayments over the previous five years but only 15 per cent thought that their *current* commitments were too high.

The OFT report speculates that this may reflect the problems faced by students in staying solvent. Credit card repayments (including store cards) had been difficult for about 41 per cent. After employment problems, the chief reason these young adults gave for repayment difficulties was that they had overcommitted themselves.

More of the twenty-five to thirty-four year olds than other age groups had taken on commitments they had later regretted and more had had difficulties repaying. The majority put this down to taking on too many commitments (compared to the other age groups who felt that unemployment or 'other' problems had been the chief cause). Credit cards had created more repayment difficulties - 31 per cent with bank credit cards, 17 per cent with store cards.

Many of these younger borrowers had stopped repayments for a time. Far fewer than in other age groups had approached their creditors to try and sort out the problem. In fact, very few had gone to any source of advice.

3.2.3 STUDENT BORROWERS

Students - largely a sub-group of the younger borrowers discussed above - are an increasingly important category of borrowers. They are marginal today, perhaps relatively affluent tomorrow. They bridge the gap between advantaged and disadvantaged borrowers and can present special problems for lenders in terms of risk assessment.

The current borrowing habits and credit experience of students are especially relevant in the light of the government's commitment to replace higher education grants with loans (15).

The OFT samples unfortunately included fewer than 2 per cent of full-time students (36 of the total sample of 2,155). Of these, just under half did not use credit currently. Out of those who did use credit, 24 per cent owed nothing and 8 per cent owed between £201 and £300. The most that was owed fell in the £3,001 to £4,000 range.

Students in the survey borrowed predominantly from banks and building societies, although credit cards were an important source of extra funds.

Although the OFT sample size is too small to be very helpful, the PAS (1987) survey, as we have seen, found a high level of repayment problems among *all* eighteen to twenty-four year olds. This may in part reflect the fact that the value of the student grant has dropped by 39 per cent in real terms since 1962, while education and living costs have soared.

The government's proposal for independent loan schemes, if implemented, will have a substantial impact on the level of student credit. We have examined the proposal and identified a number of concerns, centring on the long-term consequences of lending money to a young and marginal group of borrowers, on the likely terms of the loans, and on the methods by which lenders will assess creditworthiness.

National Union of Students estimates suggest that the debt burden for students under a loans scheme could be large. They calculated a debt of

£1,753 over a three-year degree course, rising by more than £1,000 for students in Scotland who study for four years (16). This substantial credit commitment would go up in periods of inflation if, as proposed, the loans are index-linked. Inflation was around 3 per cent at the time the government published its proposal: in late 1989 it was 7.6 per cent.

Accommodation costs can also add to student debt. The loss of housing benefit for students may increase the need for credit to underwrite rising rents. The London Housing Survey (17) found that students aged sixteen or over accounted for almost one-fifth of all those moving into privately rented accommodation in 1986/87. The average weekly rent of new private lettings was then £40.84; more than a quarter had rents over £45 a week. And although students may not always occupy rented accommodation during vacations, many are there for the full year.

More than a third of parents do not pay the full contribution to their student children assumed by the grant. Under the new proposals, local authority grants will be frozen.

There seems little doubt that credit will play an increasingly crucial role in student budgets, and judging by the PAS (1987) survey, educational attainment is no predictor of sensible credit use. More young people may be graduating with a heavy burden of credit repayments, further compounded by the need to finance a newly independent, self-supporting life. This possibility raises a number of questions. Is this paving the way for more serious, longer-term repayment difficulties? Will a heavy credit commitment prevent access to, for instance, home ownership? Will lenders offer to roll up, or consolidate, the ex-student's total credit commitments in a new, and weighted, mortgage? Would a lender be acting responsibly by offering further credit to someone with existing commitments in the region of £2,000 to £3,000 or more?

From the lenders' point of view, of course, student loan schemes may not look like a commercially prudent undertaking, given the risks. The banks and the building societies are also reluctant to bear the costs of administering repayments - which could include the costs of chasing delinquent accounts - after the student has graduated. Indeed, apart from the expense, such activities could reflect adversely on a reputation for responsible lending.

At the time of writing, the issue of who eventually is to administer and distribute the loans was still under discussion. The Bill proposed that the scheme should be administered by a private sector company, established and owned by participating institutions, under contract to the government. However, progress appeared to be very slow and although ten banks agreed to set up a company - Student Loans Company Ltd - they were only prepared to do so at no risk to themselves and with the proviso that they could withdraw at any time (18). In response to a parliamentary question in December 1989, the Secretary of State for Education announced that the banks wished to withdraw from the scheme, primarily because of the refusal of Lloyds Bank to join the proposed company. He also announced that arrangements were therefore being made for the Student Loans

Company to pass into government ownership, in order to continue preparations for the loans scheme.

A loans scheme has implications, too, for debt collection and enforcement. The government proposals suggest that student loans would be classified as a priority debt, particularly under schemes for deduction of repayments at source.

Lloyds Bank, on the other hand, has suggested a scheme aimed directly at parents and based on a secured, or equity, loan (19). This would be taken out by increasing the first mortgage and so in theory would be eligible for tax relief.

Others have proposed that the finance industry provide students with low-interest, index-linked loans (20). Debt collection problems could be eased by what would in effect be a 'garnishment' of wages from graduates.

An additional 1.5p in the £ could be added to national insurance payments; as these are already graded according to income, deductions at source would not present unfair penalties to the lower paid.

Whatever the relative merits and difficulties of a student loan scheme, these suggestions for collecting the debt certainly offer substantial administrative savings, with a greatly reduced risk of default.

3.2.4 UNEMPLOYED BORROWERS

Unemployment does not invariably bring long-term repayment problems. But unemployed people are over-represented among people taken to court for debt and among those who are disconnected from the gas or electricity for non-payment (21), who are behind with the rent (22), or who have other consumer debts. A higher than average proportion of unemployed people also appeared in the OFT's estimate of 'at-risk' groups.

In terms of the types of credit that cause repayment problems, there are variations between the short- and the longer-term unemployed. See Table III.15 *Types of credit that respondents had had difficulty repaying, by length of unemployment.*

The figures suggest that the longer a person is out of a job, the more they rely on more expensive forms of credit, such as finance company loans and credit cards.

Gillian Parker has argued that, while borrowing money is clearly associated with unemployment (especially as it becomes longer-term), this may be a *response* to financial distress rather than the main cause. She paints a vivid and credible picture:

> "... the recently unemployed household starts to take on credit, presumably for items which would previously have been bought with cash, begins to experience difficulty meeting housing costs and starts to miss fuel bills. As unemployment continues beyond twelve months the family borrows money (perhaps as a reaction to the increased amounts needed to service credit commitments), and falls into arrears with housing payments (perhaps to allow unpaid fuel bills to be met).

By the time unemployment has stretched to over twelve months, the only credit granters likely to 'take on' such families are the club and check traders who charge more for their services, thus tightening an already vicious circle." (21)

This scenario is supported by a number of research findings, including Berthoud's survey of supplementary benefit claimants in 1982 (22). Forty per cent of claimants made, or tried to make, regular credit repayments from their benefit, mostly to mail order companies (21 per cent, paying an average of £3.20 a week), followed by hire purchase, and other loan repayments (6 per cent paying an average £5.10 a week). Another 16 per cent were spending an average £2.40 a week on 'other' credit commitments. Families with children spent proportionately more of their income on credit than other claimants.

If borrowing money is indeed a *response* to being out of work, there is a strong case for ensuring extra protection for both borrowers and lenders and protecting the incomes of the unemployed. Safeguards may be needed that are aimed both at preventing repayment problems and at easing the initial stages of financial distress. The National Consumer Council has already argued the case for an examination of the system of court actions for debt (23). Lenders' default procedures - which sometimes simply precipitate further borrowing - also need looking at. We take this discussion further in section 5.

3.2.5 LOW-INCOME BORROWERS

We have already looked at the problems of low-income home buyers. Here we discuss those consumers on a low income who have *no* assets, for whom the critical issues are access to credit, and its cost.

More low-income households overall are taking on credit commitments - possibly in response to rising incomes or to wider home ownership. Between 1982 and 1986 the proportion of households making total repayments of £25 a week or more increased in nearly every income bracket. The increase was proportionately higher for lower-income groups. See Table III.16 *The percentage of households in twelve income groups making credit repayments, of £25 a week or more, 1982-86.*

Repayments of £25 a week are a substantial slice from a weekly wage of £80 to £150, leaving little leeway for a week's sickness without pay, for instance.

Few low-income borrowers in the OFT research had a bank loan. And HP/credit purchases and mail order were used far more often than credit cards (although the FES (1986) survey only records credit card use where interest payments had been made).

Surprisingly, there was very little evidence from any of the surveys of people using the *most* expensive forms of credit - moneylenders, tallymen, door-to-door salesmen. This could be due to under-reporting by respondents.

3.2.6 ELDERLY BORROWERS

People over the age of sixty-five generally know least about credit and use it less than any other age group. See Table III.17 *Elderly people's use of credit.*

Bank credit cards are the only type of credit popular with older people. Around 18 per cent of the over-sixty-fives in the PAS (1987) survey used them, and 76 per cent rated them 'convenient' (compared to 52 per cent of the total sample).

The low level of credit use among old people is related less to its cost than to attitude. More than half of the elderly people in the PAS (1987) survey said that they would not use credit and around a quarter that they could manage without it. 'Peace of mind' was given as the main reason. Of course, most are living on fixed incomes, with fixed outgoings. This balance can easily be upset by taking on the extra burden of credit repayments.

At the same time, identifiable sections of the sixty-five-plus age group are rich in terms of assets, notably a house, but poor in terms of disposable cash. Fifty per cent of people over sixty-five own their own home; some of these households are on very low incomes.

Elderly people feature high in surveys of unfit dwellings, for instance. Forty-three per cent of unfit homes in 1981 and two-thirds of homes without a bath in 1983 were occupied by retired people, many of them women on their own. Low income and failing health, combined with a lack of appropriate advice, can bring a swift deterioration in housing conditions.

Local authority home improvement grants are limited and a 1987 government consultative paper proposed means-testing applicants for these grants. Social security payments for house repairs and insurance have been replaced by repayable *loans* from the cash-limited social fund. The critical difficulties facing some elderly home owners are highlighted by recent voluntary and charitable initiatives such as the 'Care and Repair' scheme sponsored by Shelter and the Housing Associations' Charitable Trust, and the Anchor Housing Trust's 'Staying Put' scheme.

Commercial lenders have responded with a number of schemes targeted at the elderly home owner. The best known are maturity loans (an interest-only mortgage), mortgage annuity schemes (an income plan, currently held by around 40,000 people) and home reversion schemes. (These have been usefully described in detail elsewhere (24 and 25).) Most of these are available only to elderly people, and mortgage annuity plans are usually limited to people over seventy. All of them have a number of serious drawbacks.

Firstly, the schemes are complex and cumbersome, and it can be very difficult for consumers to make an informed choice before committing themselves. The income provided by a variable rate mortgage annuity scheme, for instance, fluctuates with interest rates: most borrowers therefore opt for the certainty of a fixed rate - which may initially be higher than the market standard. They are expensive to administer, particularly for

loans of less than £15,000 which fall within the
Many lenders therefore prefer only to lend amou
Indeed, the income from smaller loans is very sma
the pressure towards larger loans.

Consumers therefore depend heavily on the qualit
they receive before buying into such schemes. Ma
living alone. Although they may be competent housel
they may be inexperienced in wider or more sophisticat

Secondly, the available schemes are seldom appropria
of poor elderly people. Property that is worth less than   ,uu is
unlikely to be eligible for a commercial equity release pl   ine homes of
many old people are in need of repairs and modernisation and may not
command sufficient equity to make a loan worthwhile. Above all, the small
increase in disposable income produced by an equity release scheme can
nevertheless result in the owner losing entitlement to housing benefit, for
example.

So while the existing schemes to release the capital value of a house may
be suitable for the better-off retired home owner, they are clearly not ideal.
They may have positive disadvantages for those who are on low incomes
and entitled to means-tested benefits. Concerns have also been expressed
about the wider implications of deregulating and extending such schemes.
Organisations working with elderly people warn of the pressures that can
be brought by relatives or by authorities to borrow against the security of
a home. And many ageing people are reluctant to erode what may be their
only legacy to their children.

So although we have no objection in principle to equity release schemes,
we believe that their relationship with income support and tax concessions,
and the level of consumer safeguards and redress where there has been
abuse, do pose problems. A Building Societies Association report has
recommended more consumer-based research in the area of equity release
in old age (24). We agree. We also believe, however, that there are important
issues for borrowers who are not yet elderly, and we discuss some of these
in the next section.

3.3 Two credit products

So far in this section we have focused on problem areas from the perspective
of particular groups of *consumers*. Here we look briefly at two specific credit
products - credit cards and home equity loans - which we believe hold some
potential risks, particularly for consumers not traditionally at high risk of
getting into serious debt.

3.3.1 CREDIT CARDS AND REVOLVING CREDIT

There is no question that very many consumers appreciate the convenience
and flexibility of credit cards. Over 200 per cent more people use Access
and Visa cards today than in 1978.

also wide recognition among consumers of their pitfalls - a
that plastic cards encourage impulse-buying, and more so than any
single type of credit. (See Table III.18 *Perceived advantages and
disadvantages of credit cards)* This attitude ties in with the sort of spending
for which credit cards are commonly used - 'short-life' purchases like
clothes, petrol, entertainments, presents and travel.

One-third of the people in the OFT (1988) survey who had experienced
difficulties with *any* type of credit repayments named credit card spending
as the major problem. Almost a quarter of card users had at some time
deliberately stopped using their cards, or destroyed them. So consumers
are aware of the temptation to impulse-buy, and some consciously take
steps to put temptation out of reach.

Who are the impulsive credit card spenders? A popular view, particularly
in the media, is that they are the young and inexperienced. But this is by
no means the whole picture. Although a quarter of eighteen to twenty-four
year olds in the OFT survey had found credit card repayments most
difficult, this proportion *rose* with age.

The actual numbers of consumers who took action to stop overcommitting
themselves further were low. But their profile is interesting. The heavy
credit users who had destroyed or stopped using their cards were typically
at the younger end of the age spectrum (25-44), in social class AB, without
children under sixteen, and with an income over £15,000. And the more
money they owed, the more likely they were to have stopped using their
credit card.

There is a similar profile for those who believe credit cards encourage
impulse-buying. The least likely to hold this view were the older age groups
and those who had been unemployed for more than six months (although
this may have been a reflection of the fact that 46 per cent of this last
group had stopped using their cards).

A "typical (low income/unemployed, with young family) debtor" is very
different from the person who is likely to run into problems with credit
card repayments. Other findings have mapped out this trend towards
repayment problems among people who were originally relatively affluent.

A small study of debtors by Touche Ross (9) identified a higher than
average proportion of junior professional and skilled workers. The growing
numbers of mortgage defaulters may point to an increase in debt among
those formerly assumed to be better-off. The PAS (1987) survey confirms
that a disruption in income remains the overriding cause of repayment
difficulties. But those running into repayment difficulties chiefly as a result
of overspending on one item closely match those reporting problems with
credit cards.

Of course the figures we have drawn on only point to potential financial
trouble, not outright default. But they do demonstrate that people who are
offered credit cards and use them heavily are no more likely to be responsible
or competent in their use of credit than those who end up in court.

Precise figures on credit card bad debts are not published. Barclaycard,
with a 34 per cent share of card accounts, say that 1 per cent of their card

users encounter 'long term difficulty with debt'. This would make around 73,280 Barclaycard account holders (1988 figures).

The role of credit cards in overall credit commitment, and overcommitment, is not overwhelming. They are a popular and flexible way of borrowing money. But they attach a marked burden of personal responsibilities to the user and - as both users and non-users recognise - they have the *potential* to encourage overspending. This is of some concern and in section 5 we make some recommendations for extra safeguards for the more vulnerable credit card consumers.

3.3.2 ASSET-BASED AND HOME EQUITY LENDING

Mortgages now account for some 80 per cent of personal borrowing in the UK. One estimate puts the potential secured lending market at around £378 billion (26). We have already commented on the trend towards lending against property for more ephemeral spending and for a longer duration (see section 1). Following on from this, lenders are now starting to develop new types of secured lending, targeted at what they see as low-risk customers - the more affluent home owner.

Home equity loans, like simple mortgages, are secured against property. they allow up to 80 per cent of the capital value of a house to be converted to credit, often using a cheque book or credit card. The market is still in its early days in this country but it is highly developed in the United States and Canada and, more recently, in Australia. We base much of our comment in this section on experience in those countries.

Unlike a first mortgage, home equity loans promote the attractions of consumption rather than investment. They combine the ease of a credit card or cheque book with a large, almost open-ended credit source, and allow substantial sums to be borrowed against an extendable personal credit ceiling: this is especially so when property prices are buoyant. The repayment arrangements for home equity loans, like those for other revolving credit, are overtly simple and flexible.

However, there are serious risks for consumers in a scheme that pledges your home against instant credit. Home equity loans often include deferred payment arrangements which can prolong the borrower's commitment almost indefinitely. They are subject to unlimited interest rate rises - an acute problem in times of rising inflation. And since the lender is acquiring maximum security, there may be less care taken to assess the borrower's capacity to handle the loan sensibly, or to repay it.

A recent survey by the Consumer Union and the Consumer Federation of America concluded that home equity loans were the biggest single threat to the financial well-being of consumers:

> ".... because [they] are a unique combination of several traditional credit features that, together, multiply the borrower risk inherently associated with personal debt." (27)

As a result of consumer pressure in the US, Congress passed the *Home Equity Consumer Protection Act*, which came into effect in November 1989 and which sets clear protective guidelines for consumers taking on these forms of loan.

A market has already been launched in this country. We have already mentioned proposals for commercial 'educational lending' (section 3.2.3), to pay for students through higher education, for instance. Property-owning parents are an obvious target for home equity lending. We have also discussed the potential expansion among elderly home-owners (section 3.2.6).

Indeed secured lending has attractions for both lenders and borrowers. From the lender's point of view, the risk is securely covered with a large, and usually appreciating, capital asset. The bigger the loan and the longer its term, the more profitable it is to the creditor. For the consumer, such a loan releases cash from an otherwise non-liquid asset and offers simple, flexible access and repayment.

But borrowers under these schemes are taking on a huge burden of risk. They can spend freely on anything from a child's college fees to cars, holidays and food, and in the process whittle away at valuable capital. The risk of rapid overcommitment, even insolvency, is evident. Equally serious, although largely beyond the scope of this review, are the larger economic questions that go with erosion of a major capital base.

Home equity loans are set to expand. It is a form of consumer credit about which we have serious concerns.

3.4 How do consumers select their credit?

An important question - since the answer has an impact on every stage of the commitment to repay - is: how do consumers make their borrowing decisions? At its simplest, we might predict that two key forces drive most such decisions - need and cost. We start with the factor on which the National Consumer Council made recommendations ten years ago: consumer awareness of the costs of credit.

3.4.1 THE PRICE OF CREDIT

In our 1980 report *Consumers and Credit* we reported that consumers were confused about the real, and relative, costs of borrowing. They seemed unable to assess them. In that report we urged the wide use of a single yardstick to make calculations and comparisons simpler and fair - the annual percentage rate, or APR.

Does the information that is now available about APRs actually influence how people decide?

According to the PAS survey seven years later, only one in five consumers could say what APR stood for, and even fewer could explain what it meant. Over half the men in the survey did not know. Two in three women did not know, and half could not even make a guess at its meaning. Ignorance was highest at each end of the age spectrum, in social class DE and among the unemployed and retired.

The borrowers who *had* thought about price (APR) were more likely also to have had problems over repayment (53 per cent, compared to 44 per cent of those who had not had problems). So perhaps an unhappy experience makes people pay more attention to the cost of credit. But even among the consumers who had given some consideration to price, their estimates of the APR on credit cards and bank and finance house loans were wildly variable, most apparently amounting to guesswork.

All this casts some doubt on the case we made in 1980 that - given time and publicity - consumers would begin readily to understand and use APR as a measure of costs when making their borrowing decisions. This does not appear to have happened. Why not?

Perhaps it is not surprising that people are vague about how the calculation is made. It is the kind of formula that most of us forget as soon as we leave school: this is just one of three official formulae—

$$APR = 100 \frac{[(1 + \frac{x}{100})^y - 1]}{}$$

x is the monthly/period rate of charge expressed as a percentage
y is the number of times in a year the period rate of charge is applied
   (twelve, for example, if the charges are monthly)

There may perhaps have been too much stress laid on *understanding* APR, and not enough on *using* it.

It is undeniably important that people first understand that a high APR may cost them more than a low APR.

The next crucial consideration - and this seems to be less well grasped - is the *length of repayment*. If consumers were encouraged to use this as a measure, they may then begin to understand that although the APR may be a high one, repaying the debt over a short period may actually cost them less overall than a low APR repaid over a much longer period. For example:

Amount of loan	Monthly repayment	Total repayment
APR 19.5 per cent £1,000	over 12 months £91.68	£1,100.16
	over 24 months £49.92	£1,198.08
	over 60 months £25.39	£1,523.40
APR 16.7 per cent £1,000	over 60 months £24.11	£1,446.60

There is some evidence that people *may* now be starting to use the APR when taking out certain sorts of loan. One of the trends identified in this report (section 3.3.2) is that towards loans secured on property. This means a lower APR and, if APR on its own is the consideration, seems as good a deal.

However, the length of the repayment (plus the fact that your home is pledged as security) means that borrowers may not be getting as good a deal as they think. The trend is also likely to reflect the fact that lenders are accepting a much wider range of customers than before: in 1980 we noted that people on a tight budget had little option but to choose loans with small repayments over a long period even though the total cost of the credit would eventually be more.

We believe more research into the way borrowers choose their credit, particularly when they decide on secured loans, is urgently needed.

Consumers may also have become confused by the two different ways in which interest charges are presented to them. The charge may be pre-arranged, as in the example above: this is typically the case for a bank or finance house loan. Or it may be presented as a charge on the outstanding balance of a loan, most commonly on credit card loans, where the amount outstanding is not necessarily known at the outset.

This difference in presentation is important. Before the introduction of credit cards, most borrowers expected to be clear about the total charge for credit at the time they took out a loan. Our 1980 survey found that hire purchase (probably including all types of fixed sum instalment credit) was used by more people at some time than any other form of credit. This was particularly true among younger people, non-skilled manual workers, and those in middle-income brackets.

By the time of the 1987 PAS survey, the picture had changed. While the profile of credit users is similar, only 5 per cent said they were currently using hire purchase and only 4 per cent credit sale. Credit cards have probably replaced these.

So people who ten years ago were often using fixed-sum credit, with 'transparent' interest charges worked out in advance, have changed their borrowing habits. They are now using far more revolving and running-account credit in which the method of charging is not so obvious to them. This is particularly true for credit cards used for extended credit. Some credit cards make daily interest charges on the loan, others on the monthly outstanding balance. This gives more emphasis to the minimum monthly repayment figure - which is familiar, relatively constant and predictable. But it is not a sound guide to the borrower of their credit costs in the long term.

We still believe that the APR is a valuable yardstick for assessing credit costs. Clearly, however, it is not as easy to use if borrowers are taking extended credit on their credit cards. In section 5.4 we make some general recommendations for helping these borrowers. Here we consider some of the other factors, apart from cost, that influence the choice of credit.

3.4.2 OTHER, NON-PRICE, CONSIDERATIONS

Although the cost of a loan - interest paid and overall 'price' - is one influence on choice, consumers take other measures into account. How you apply for the loan, its flexibility and convenience, the length of the repayment period, the *size* of the repayments as well as how they are made - these are all non-price considerations that have a bearing on people's selection. The social fund, for example, offers loans at no extra cost but take-up of these loans is only now increasing after an initial surprisingly low demand. Need and demand are unlikely to have declined dramatically in the year or so after social fund loans were introduced. Other factors must be operating.

Consumers' views about the advantages and disadvantages of the most popular form of credit - the credit card - are instructive. It seems that 'price' may have a fairly low ranking in the decision to use a card (only 11 per cent of people in the OFT survey agreed that it was cheaper to use than other types of credit). The table below ranks the level of response on credit cards against fourteen other types of commercially available credit.

Perceived advantage	Percentage agreeing	Ranking out of 15
	%	
You don't have to have personal contact with the supplier	33	1
You can pay as much or as little of what you owe as and when you wish	33	1
You only have to make the minimum payment	41	1
It's easy to obtain	38	2
You can usually increase your limit if you request it	35	1
You can pay off all you owe at once if you wish	42	1

Source: PAS (1987)

So users see the credit card as flexible, convenient, impersonal and adaptable. Only mail order is perceived as an easier form of credit to obtain. (Flexibility can however, be a double-edged sword, especially for people on a tight budget - and 68 per cent of people agreed that a credit card encourages impulse-buying.)

One reason why consumers rate credit cards highly is because they do not involve personal contact with the lender. An interview to discuss borrowing money (like a "chat with the bank manager") induces anxiety and even guilt in many people: this instinct is compounded if people perceive a censorious or unfeeling attitude on the lender's part, as may be true even for *interest-free* social fund loans.

The special psychology attached to shopping for credit was vividly described by Packard in *The Hidden Persuaders* back in 1957:

> "His [Dr Dichter's] particular interest was in the paradox of the great growth of loan companies in spite of the fact that most banks were offering personal loans at a lower interest rate and were more lenient in accepting people for loans. His conclusion was that the loan company's big advantage over the bank is in its lower moral tone!
>
> The bank's big handicap is its stern image as a symbol of unemotional morality. We are asking this personification of virtue to condescend to take a chance on us frail humans. In contrast, when we go to a loan company for a loan, it is we who are the virtuous ones and the loan company is the villain we are temporarily forced to consort with. Here it is we, the borrowers, who do the condescending. Dr Dichter explains: 'This shift in moral dominance from lender to borrower completely changes the whole emotional undertone of the transaction. We shift from feeling like an unreliable adolescent to feeling like a morally righteous adult. The higher cost of the loan is a small price to pay for such a great change in outlook." (*Reproduced by permission of John Farquharson Ltd. Copyright Vance Packard 1957.*) (28)

So although a better public understanding of APR is, we believe, an important objective, it has to be recognised that other influences can overrule the shopper's 'logical' (or cheapest) choice when it comes to buying credit. It is in this context that we turn to other influences on consumer choice - the availability of information about credit, and how products are advertised and promoted.

3.4.3 INFORMATION AND ADVICE ABOUT CREDIT

For credit, as for other goods and services, consumers depend on sound information to make sensible buying decisions.

Between 1987/88 and 1988/89, spending by the top ten financial institutions on advertising increased by 33 per cent. American Express Europe (Card Division) virtually tripled its spending to £8.3 million, chiefly on the launch of its Optima credit card. Total spending on advertising by the financial sector in 1988/89 was around £150,000 million (29).

Meanwhile, the independent organisations offering money advice and information to consumers were very poorly funded. The budget for the entire citizens' advice network in England and Wales for 1988/89 was £9.3 million, for instance. Debt counsellors and money advisers cumulatively received around £1.4 million (including £250,000 from industry sources). The Money Management Council - an independent charity promoting education and better understanding of personal finance - had an annual budget of about £100,000. The Office of Fair Trading publishes some booklets on credit and debt and some newspapers offer specific advice.

It is fair to say that advertising and promotion by the industry is the most visible and accessible source of information on finance for consumers. What does this information tell them?

Although credit advertisements are selling money, they seldom put it so bluntly. They tend to deal with image and with the purchases that credit will make available, moulded to the aspirations of their target audience. Credit card advertising, in particular, promotes discretionary spending and, as we have seen, overcommitment is more common on credit cards than for other types of borrowing. Similarly, advertisements for the new type of equity loan (discussed in section 3.3.2) - aimed predominantly at better-off home owners and those who are well into repaying their mortgages - emphasise that these secured loans are ideal for short-term, short-life purchases like holidays.

The OFT survey showed that 79 per cent of people agreed that there should be tighter controls on the advertising of credit.

In 1987 we published *Security Risks*, which reviewed all the advertisements for secured loans for purposes such as home improvements or (of special concern) to pay off other debts to appear in the national press in one week. Most of the ads were placed by brokers rather than by financial institutions, and were targeted at consumers already in financial distress. We described many of the advertisements as seriously misleading both about the security for the loans and about the high - sometimes extortionate - rates of interest. Althought the government subsequently tightened the regulations on credit advertisements, this type of lending is still heavily promoted.

3.4.4 ASSESSING RISK

In section 4 we investigate credit risk assessment by lenders, and its efficiency as a way of preventing bad debts, in some detail. But it is relevant, too, to our discussion here about consumers' attitudes to buying credit, and about whether people shop around before they buy.

The new streamlined systems of risk assessment used by lenders have helped to extend access to credit to many more customers. The old methods (like written references), often subjective and judgemental, have been replaced by statistically sophisticated measures called credit scoring.

Credit scoring systems are designed to assess the likelihood that the borrower will repay the loan. They analyse the information given at the time of application. (Additional information about bad debts or recorded loan default is usually collected separately, through a credit reference agency, also discussed in detail in section 4.)

A typical application form will ask for:

occupation
number of years in present employment
banking status/length of time with bank
accommodation status
time at current address

age and marital status

number of children

telephone number

Although lenders may ask about an applicant's other regular credit commitments, like mortgage/rent and store accounts, this information is not regarded by lenders as 'predictive' for the purposes of risk assessment.

So the lender is measuring *stability* and *dependability* - the statistical likelihood of the applicant making stable and regular repayments.

What is missing from automated risk assesment, however, is any real measure of an applicant's *capacity* to repay - in other words, his or her income and how far the household budget is *already* stretched. The fact that an applicant for a loan may already be overcommitted can be masked.

The assessment system for a revolving credit account is a case in point. On application for a storecard (the major users of credit scoring systems) or other credit card, the system isolates and assesses the applicant's 'stability factors'. The same is true of systems that monitor accounts while they are being repaid. Provided the borrower is making regular repayments, irrespective of how small the amount is, this is sufficient demonstration to the lender that the borrower is reliable and dependable. All well and good. But it may also mean that the borrower's budget is already heavily committed, a factor that credit scoring, used alone, disregards.

The PAS (1987) survey showed that the credit card limits of eighteen to twenty-four year olds tended to be between £100 and £599, and between £900 to £1,999 for older age groups. One in four people had more than one card. Multiple use was commoner among higher-income twenty-five to forty-four year olds and social groups AB and C1. As we have already seen, these are also the groups most commonly reporting repayment difficulties and overcommitment on their credit cards.

Users may be making minimum-only repayments on their outstanding commitments, so that the real extent of any repayment difficulties is masked. Some will have reached their upper credit limit and be making "interest-only" repayments, thus paying off very little of the loan capital and, often, rapidly increasing the outstanding commitment.

The exclusion of financial capacity from the scoring system can have serious consequences for borrowers. It takes no account of the individual who has already borrowed up to the hilt.

A credit transaction is of course a joint contract between borrower and lender. Consumers have a choice about whether or not to enter into the agreement. But it is widely held - and many lenders acknowledge this - that the balance of the responsibility must tip towards those lending their own, or their investors', money. This has implications from a social and educational point of view. It also places a burden on the lenders to develop and use sensitive and responsible marketing and risk assessment methods.

Sophisticated credit scoring, while improving consumer access to credit, has also underpinned the lenders' commercial drive to capture customers before they move to a competitor. It has promoted the idea of "instant access", encouraging consumers to believe they have a "right" to credit (and to be offended when it is refused). And, as we have seen (and discuss again in section 4), it operates to maximise the lenders' business but not to identify those people whose small "£s per week" are mounting into an unmanageable overload.

We look to lenders to take more responsibility for reducing consumer credit difficulties, by emphasising to their customers the *joint* nature of the credit contract, by emphasising the future consequences of signing a credit application today, and by giving serious consideration to an applicant's income when deciding whether or not to grant a loan.

References to section 3

1. Janet Ford, *The Indebted Society: credit and default in the 1980s*, Routledge, 1988.
2. Building Societies Association, "The characteristics of building society borrowers in 1988", *Housing Finance*, no. 2, April 1989.
3. Reward Group, "Cost of living - regional comparisons March 1989", cited in the *Independent*, 7 April 1989.
4. Glen Bramley, *Access to Owner-occupation*, research note prepared for the Association of District Councils, August 1988.
5. *Hansard*, 26.11.87, col.304.
6. Department of the Environment, *Living in Temporary Accommodation: a survey of homeless people*, by Andrew Thomas and Pat Niner, HMSO, 1989.
7. London Business School, *Economic Outlook 1987-1991*, vol.12 (10), July 1988.
8. Peter Warburton, "Facts and trends in EFT and consumer credit", speech to the *Cards on Table* conference, London, 1988.
9. Touche Ross Management Consultants, *Study of Debt Enforcement Procedures*, carried out for the Civil Justice Review, Lord Chancellor's Department, December 1986.
10. R. Cotterrell and others, 'The recovery of judgement debts in the county court: some preliminary results', in I. Ramsay (ed.), *Debtors and Creditors*, Professional Books, 1986.
11. Jubilee Centre, *Families in Debt: the nature, causes and effects of debt problems and policy proposals for their alleviation*, research paper no.7, 1988.
12. Michael Adler, "The economic and social situation of consumer debtors in Great Britain", in G. Hormann (ed.), *Verbraucherkredit und Verbraucherinsolvenz, Bremen*, 1986.
13. J. Gregory and J. Monk, *Survey of Defenders in Court Actions in Scotland*, research report for the Scottish Law Commission, no. 6, HMSO, 1981.
14. National Association of Citizens Advice Bureaux, *Dealing with Debt*, a report on the first year's progress of NACAB's Greater Manchester/East Cheshire Money Advice Project, 1989.
15. Department of Education and Science, *Top-up Loans for Students*, HMSO, 1988, Cm 520.

16. National Union of Students, *Submission to the Department of Education and Science concerning the Government White Paper "Top-up loans for students"*, NUS, 1989.

17. London Research Centre, *Access to Housing in London*, a report based on the results of the London Housing Survey 1986-87, LRC, April 1988.

18. "Wrong questions do not produce the right answer", *Independent*, 23 November 1989, p.21.

19. "Student loans: a better way", *Lloyds Bank Economic Review*, no. 122, February 1989.

20. "Why the government is wrong on student loans", *Independent*, 12 January 1989, p.15.

21. Gillian Parker, "Unemployment, low income and debt" in I. Ramsay (ed.), *Debtors and Creditors*, Professional Books, 1986.

22. Richard Berthoud, *The Reform of Supplementary Benefit*, Policy Studies Institute, 1984.

23. National Consumer Council, *Ordinary Justice: legal services and the courts in England and Wales*, HMSO, 1989.

24. Philip Leather and Rose Wheeler, *Making Use of Home Equity in Old Age*, Building Societies Association, 1988.

25. A. Fleiss, *Home Ownership Alternatives for the Elderly*, HMSO, 1985.

26. Mark Boleat and Adrian Coles, *The Mortgage Market*, Allen & Unwin, 1988.

27. Consumers Union and Consumer Federation of America, *Testimony to US Congress on HR 3011, the Home Equity Consumer Protection Act of 1987*.

28. Vance Packard, *The Hidden Persuaders*, Longmans, 1957.

29. Campaign, *Top 100 Advertisers*, 1989, p.18.

4. The decision to lend:
credit granting and risk assessment

Moneylending involves the risk that the money will not be repaid. To reduce this risk, most lenders make some assessment of the suitability of the people who apply for loans. With the unprecedented expansion in personal borrowing in the last ten years - and in the competitive edge between lenders - the old system of taking up references was too slow, cumbersome and unreliable. It became essential for financial institutions to respond very quickly to consumer demand without at the same time raising the odds on default.

So since 1980, side by side with the growth in lending, there have been changes in the methods by which lenders quantify the risks they are taking. Automated 'credit scoring', identity checks, and computerised searches of shared information on credit agreements are all now being used to help lenders to test the probability of full repayment, on time, of the credit they offer.

This automation has brought consumer benefits. It has substantially improved people's access to credit and, to a lesser but still marked extent, it has prevented the level of default rocketing at the same level as new credit.

But to most borrowers, how their suitability for a loan is assessed is a mystery. Only those who are refused a loan generally query the system. There are notions of a vast computer holding a credit 'blacklist', and nagging fears that lenders are collecting and storing inaccurate and potentially damaging information, and intruding on individual privacy.

It is clear, too, that the assessment methods that are being used let through some bad risks. The rate of growth in default has certainly been lower than the rate of growth in credit, but the number of casualties and the extent of their commitments are still alarmingly high.

In this section we take a close look at risk assessment. We examine how the commonest methods actually work. We look at the winners and the losers under these systems, and discuss ways in which all the institutions granting credit could help to make consumer access fairer while reducing the risks to themselves and to their customers. In the last part of the section, we examine the ambivalent attitudes of consumers to credit referencing as it operates now and report on the safeguards that have been introduced into the business in other countries.

4.1 The systems used to assess risk

The industry uses a number of tools to decide whether or not to lend money to a consumer. There are three basic steps: checking identity and address; checking for county court judgements recorded against the applicant; and searching for other information on the applicant's credit commitments, past and present.

The first two checks are often the basic "credit reference". The third is a more thorough look at the borrower's record. This one will depend upon the lender being a subscriber to the more detailed (and confidential) databases; it will also vary according to the level of checking the lender wants to carry out - all the checks involve an agency fee. Small lenders may be less willing to bear these extra costs. We have taken the phrase "credit referencing" to include all the searches - the optimal situation. In addition, a lender may make use of all these categories of information to calculate a "credit score" on an application.

4.1.1 CREDIT REFERENCING

This is the first and most important check on a loan applicant. It involves:
★ verifying the applicant's identity;
★ searching for county court judgements recorded against the applicant's address in the previous six years; and
★ searching for any existing shared information about a past or current credit record.

The overall volume of information needed to run these checks is massive, demanding expensive computer hardware and appropriate software. As a result, as credit has expanded, large and sophisticated credit reference agencies have developed to handle the job for lenders.

Credit reference agencies operate under a licence from the Office of Fair Trading. Over 7,570 licences have been issued, but the sector is dominated by the three largest agencies - Infolink, CCN Systems Ltd, and Westcot Data Ltd - which control 90 per cent of the market between them (1).

While credit referencing is the agencies' basic service and provides the bread and butter of turnover, they are developing other services: direct marketing, geodemographic profiling, international services, business data and overdue accounts collection are major growth areas. The confidential credit information is kept separate and distinct from these other services.

4.1.2 THE CONSUMER DATABASE

This is the information held by credit reference agencies and supplied to lenders. Despite some public apprehension, the database only holds factual data. The files do not, for instance, hold a "credit rating" on individuals. It is up to the lenders who buy the service to analyse the data and to make their own lending decisions.

Stored in the databases are three categories of information.

The first offers a basic identity check. The three largest agencies hold on computer the 44.2 million names on the electoral register, updated twice a year. The lender will get confirmation of forename, surname, full postal address and length of residence. (In section 4.4.1 below, we discuss the flaws in this identity check system.)

The second category of information are county court (but not high court) judgements, bankruptcies and data on serious default. County court judgement debts are compiled centrally by the Registry Trust, a non-profitmaking organisation set up by the Lord Chancellor's Office. Information is held on file for six years after the judgement. Information on debts written off without going to court - "default data" - is held on most files for three years.

When a lender asks for a check, the credit reference agency searches for judgement debts registered *against a specific address*. The answer goes to the lender irrespective of the name under which the debt is registered. This may therefore include "third party information" (examined below, in section 4.4). This check also tells the lender about previous searches by other lenders, but not whether those loans were approved or not.

At the third, most detailed level, lenders subscribing to the database can ask for a full credit reference. This is more expensive. The largest agencies keep "closed user" (access by subscribers only) databases which record details of current and recent consumer credit agreements, information that many of the largest lenders voluntarily share with each other. It is supplied by subscribers to the agency monthly, on magnetic tape, and covers up-to-date details on new credit agreements and payment histories of customers over the previous twelve months.

Subscriber-only information includes credit transaction details - both adverse information, for instance that an account is in arrears, and positive, for instance that an account has been repaid regularly.

Only those contributing information - and therefore only licensed lenders - have access to these files. Appendix IV.1 gives a voluntary code of practice to which lenders may be asked to abide.

The sort of information provided on a full credit reference is in Appendix IV.2. It reveals only factual details, number coded. If any judgements are registered for the address, these are shown. There are no statements of opinion, and no details of current/savings accounts held, telephone, fuel or power debts, or mortgage/rent arrears. We discuss these gaps in the information in section 4.2.1 below.

4.1.3 CREDIT SCORING

Credit scoring was developed in the United States in the early 1960s and came here in the mid-1970s. It is now used by all the major lenders. The major push in development came from the large retail credit card operators, and it has been used increasingly by others such as Access and Visa members and the building societies.

It is a rapid statistical system for (a) assessing the probability that an applicant for a loan will repay the money owed and (b) setting the level of risk the creditor is currently prepared to tolerate in its own lending decisions. Each system - involving "scorecards" - is tailored to the individual organisation, reflecting its own customer groups, risk levels and past lending experience. Using credit scoring to make lending decisions can increase the number of approvals, reduce bad debts, cut investigation costs and generally improve a supplier's lending portfolio. It also provides management information useful to a lender in responding to market changes.

At the same time, credit scoring has its limitations and is by no means infallible. Building a scorecard is a lengthy and skilled process. It is expensive - costing around £30,000 to £35,000 to develop. One scorecard has a typical lifespan of only around three years and many large lenders use up to twenty different scorecards at any one time. The statistical information they contain needs close monitoring and updating as market conditions change.

How does credit scoring work?

Scorecards vary in design but in practice are all based on a combination of information and a calculation of odds. This produces a ready reckoner against which to measure applications for loans.

The information used in assembling a scorecard is:
★ information on completed application forms;
★ information from credit reference agency files; and
★ (usually) any available third party information, such as debts of a spouse or other family member. Usually, this is publicly available information, typically from county court judgement records.

This information is compiled for a large sample of customers (around 4,500) over at least two to three years. The sample needs to include equal numbers of "good", "bad" and "rejected" loan customers.

The odds are computed in a cascade system, drawing in more variables to refine the discrimination until "breakeven" - theoretically ideal - odds are reached. With this the lender calculates the number of good payers needed to balance the losses from the predicted number of bad payers. The final stage is to produce an algorithm that transforms the predictive value of the selected variables (such as age, employment, years at one address, accommodation status, etc.) from a probability expression into a single score for a single applicant.

The breakeven point is different for different sectors of the industry. It varies according to the level of risk they are prepared to take, the level of bad debt they can absorb, and the profile of their customers. One creditor may accept breakeven odds of 3 to 1 (that is, one bad payer for every three good accounts), another will take 5 to 1. Whatever the odds, applicants producing scores below a lender's breakeven point will be rejected. However, an applicant rejected by one creditor's criteria may well be accepted by another's.

Sometimes the customer sample may produce particular correlation effects. Women may be over-represented, or home owners. To compensate for this, some variables are weighted. This corrects distortions but also enables the best discriminators of risk to be isolated. So from a huge mass of variables, a scorecard can be refined to the most significant predictors of risk.

It is important to note that no *single* variable - sex, age, employment status, gender or address - will produce an automatic thumbs-down from a scorecard. Indeed a properly constructed scorecard should eliminate sex discrimination and so-called "red-lining" (a refusal of credit because of the area in which the applicant lives). The deciding factor is the *overall score*, arising out of a combination of variables which genuinely reflect the characteristics of the total sample of credit users. So the system is designed to be unbiased and non-judgemental.

Credit scoring enables lenders to maximise the number of loans they accept according to their own risk criteria. But it is not a failsafe system. It cannot predict sudden illness, unemployment, death or marital breakdown - the commonest causes of default. It cannot ensure that all the customers whom lenders accept will be good payers. And it will reject some applicants who would have been reliable. The level of "false positives" and "false negatives" will depend on the variables used, the cut-off score for acceptances and, significantly, the use of any third party information in the calculation. Appendix IV.3 shows a hypothetical example of some scorecard variables.

New developments in credit scoring

As more people become regular borrowers, more information is available to lenders and, through this, new ways of assessing risk.

Performance scoring is one important new way. It developed from scorecard techniques, but instead of testing risk at the point when someone applies for credit, it examines an existing account, and how it is being maintained, as a way of predicting how that customer is likely to service accounts in the future.

Performance scoring systems are designed to enable lenders:
★ to improve the targeting, timing and effectiveness of their default and collection procedures;
★ to identify accounts that seem to be running into difficulties and set controls on these customers' credit limits; and
★ to identify healthy accounts, and maximise their profitability by targeting more promotions and services at these customers.

The system takes into account how much of a bill is paid, when and by what method, and other details of customer payment. Samples of creditors and uncreditworthy accounts are used, often collected at various times of year to avoid seasonal bias. About one in four of the sample is set aside to test the final model: this is crucial, to assess the performance scorecard's practical ability to predict "good" and "bad" accounts.

The system benefits the lender by making the most of their best customers and identifying those with account problems. It has some potential problems from the consumer point of view which we return to below.

4.2 How effective are risk assessment systems?

The figures for consumer debt in the 1980s make sombre reading.

Court action against defaulters by banks and finance houses have quadrupled since 1980. County court actions for recovery of money or land rose from 1.3 million in 1979 to nearly 2.4 million in 1987. We have already charted the figures for fuel disconnections (section 2.5), rent and mortgage arrears (section 2.5 and 3.1.1) and other consumer debts.

These statistics represent the serious casualties of debt. Without risk assessment the figures would probably be even worse. Nonetheless, it is arguable that the more sophisticated the techniques become, the greater the margin of risk that the lender is prepared to take - with the greater risk being weighted against the borrower who perhaps should not have been given more credit. Again, until financial capacity to absorb the repayment, along with other commitments, is included in scoring and assessment, the greatest risk will often be carried by the borrower.

A high proportion of debt casualties arise through personal crises like marital breakdown, illness or unemployment. These are generally *un*predictable. But another part of the equation lies in the limitations of the information used to assess risk. The range of data, although large, omits some significant material. Furthermore, not all lenders participate in sharing information or using credit reference agency searches.

4.2.1 GAPS IN THE DATA

The information about arrears filed with credit reference agencies is largely confined to consumer credit agreements past and present. It does not include gas, electricity or water debts nor mortgage and rent arrears. We have seen that these are often warning signals of financial distress. A household may be diverting money for these bills, to pay what they feel to be even more pressing debts.

The National Consumer Council sees advantages in including fuller information on arrears and default (so-called "black information") in risk assessment systems. In particular, it would shape the system into more of a preventive tool than it is at present. Additional data would help to pinpoint more accurately those already struggling to meet household commitments and for whom more credit would bring worse financial problems. It would give a fuller picture of the capacity of an applicant to cope with a new loan, in terms of their income/debt ratio - in other words, how far their budget is already stretched.

However, the extra information needed to achieve this more rounded profile would be vast. Among other data, it would mean adding to agency files:

★ 46,370 mortgage borrowers in arrears of more than six months (at the end of 1988);

★ 78,569 people disconnected from their electricity supply (in 1988-89);

★ 61,769 people disconnected from their gas supply (in the twelve months to March 1988);

★ almost half the entire local authority rent accounts in inner city and metropolitan areas (the estimate of those in arrears) plus around 270,000 people in arrears with their housing association lets;

★ a minimum of 7,000 people (in England and Wales) disconnected for non-payment of water rates (in 1987-88) ;

★ an estimated 1,212,000 people summonsed for nonpayment of rates (in the twelve months to March 1986).

Default details like these are, we believe, even more pertinent to assessing the risk of financial overcommitment than the data used now. A variety of research findings (2) and evidence from money advisers and debt counsellors show that borrowers often pay their contractual consumer credit debts, however small, before the bills for utility services, rent or even mortgages.

The sheer volume of this information of course has cost and resource implications for credit reference agencies. However, we understand that it is now technically feasible. Apart from the logistical problems of staff and data-handling, the law properly requires that information like this is kept accurately and up-to-date. Furthermore, very clear guidelines would be needed about the point at which information about a consumer's arrears passed from the creditor to the database.

It is possible that further refinements in performance scoring will go some way towards more reliable predictions of financial casualty, by making better use of the existing database information (see below).

Meanwhile, there is one category of debt that we believe could and should be added immediately to risk assessment systems: all default on secured lending.

In earlier chapters we have described the massive growth in secured lending - both first mortgages and other loans secured against people's homes. Consumers are being encouraged to exchange capital value for instant cash. We have noted too the easier access to credit for owner-occupiers, even when existing levels of indebtedness are high, and the suspicion that creditors may be increasingly inclined to rely on the security of a house to mask poor lending decisions.

Our 1987 report *Security Risks* (3) described the worrying level of problems among consumers who take out some types of secured loans, notably through finance brokers. Some of the problems were due to ignorance and financial naivety. But a significant number were due to exploitation of people who were already heavily financially committed and desperate to borrow more.

Members of the Finance Houses Association have been important contributors to credit reference agencies for some years. Working with Infolink, they helped to establish a Payment Profile Service for members, and almost all members subscribe information to this database or the CAIS system operated by CCN. Much of this contains details of secured loans made by FHA members. However, secured lending by banks and building societies is not available.

The case for adding information on serious mortgage arrears and comprehensive information on default on other secured lending to credit reference databases is, we believe, a powerful one.

There is some debate about extending the need for another, quite different, category of information to be shared among lenders - so-called "white information". This already happens to an extent through lenders pooling and sharing information on the conduct of their consumer credit agreements - for example, store card accounts and finance house loans. The other types of "white information" include, for example, agreed overdrafts and other kinds of unsecured bank or building society loan.

There appears to be substantial consumer resistance to this proposal. There are also problems for the lenders, both technical and commercial - the relevant institutions are reluctant to share customer details like these with their competitors. If the suppliers cannot trust their fellow subscribers to use this kind of information fairly, it is hardly surprising that consumers are worried. In some EEC countries, Holland for instance, *all* bona fide consumer credit agreements are required to be registered with an agency. Such a system would certainly throw up a great many instances of multiple debt and has much to commend it. However, extending "white information" to agreed overdrafts and other personal account details would not, we believe, significantly reduce default and credit casualty.

Even if *all* the information we have outlined were available to lenders, some borrowers would still face disaster. Financial difficulty in a household remains, by and large, unpredictable - unemployment, marital breakdown, sickness and death strike indiscriminately. We believe that the information now acquired through loan application forms, plus the existing (albeit limited) information on default, are adequate, if not perfect, for credit scoring. Extending one provision on the use of "black" (arrears and default) information would help. Developments in performance scoring should also give lenders a better idea of whether or not to lend more to existing borrowers.

4.2.2 GAPS AMONG THE PROVIDERS OF INFORMATION

Participation in credit reference schemes is not universal. A number of finance houses and retailers do not take part. Some building societies do not place unsecured loans on file, although since May 1988 banks have been lodging information on delinquent accounts. Very many smaller lenders - often dealing with high risk or unsophisticated borrowers - will not use, nor provide, information. The public utilities and local authorities are not involved.

Completely comprehensive data is technically challenging and, as we have suggested, not necessarily the answer. But we believe that all lenders should be strongly encouraged to share information of the kind now recorded on databases and, in particular, that building societies and others making secured loans should share their files on arrears and default. Needless to say, information should be shared only for the purposes of risk assessment, and consumers should be kept informed about the process.

4.3 Is the existing data used effectively?

As we have seen, although outstanding consumer credit has risen dramatically, the available evidence on outright debt and default does not show an equivalent growth rate. The way in which consumer data is used to gauge applications for credit has, we believe, contributed to this and improved overall levels of default.

However, this trend has predominantly been to the benefit of lenders and creditors. We are not convinced that the data is used in a way that significantly affects the potential for *overcommitment* by individual borrowers. Multiple indebtedness is commonplace, according to the Office of Fair Trading's 1988 findings, to information from debt counsellors and advice agencies, and to evidence from creditors themselves (4).

We have already suggested that lenders may be relying more and more on high-value security to compensate for high-risk lending and argued for the inclusion of all secured loans in risk assessment. Here we look at another weakness in credit scoring - the way it measures individual risk.

The lending institutions undoubtedly give more responsible consideration to their lending decisions than in the past. We applaud this. But their first responsibility is of course to their shareholders, and it is a commercial fact of life that controlled arrears can be profitable.

Interest payments on interest owing substantially increase the profit on loans. Fast repayments give a lower return. So stable but slow repayers are both the bread and butter, and the jam, of the credit industry. Their credit scoring systems reflect this. Initial credit scoring concentrates chiefly on the probability of repayment. Evidence of *stable* repayment is highly rated by lenders, whatever the total length or amount. A person's *total* commitment is not necessarily treated as an important variable. Nor is the credit *limit* that is tied to their credit cards.

While financial regularity rather than financial capacity is the lenders' chief concern, the sort of delinquent account portfolios illustrated in the box on the next page will continue.

Mr and Mrs A, the Wirral			
Access	£1,959	Royal Bank of Scotland	£67
Bank of Scotland	1,395	Trustcard	800
Barclaycard	1,754	TSB	1,200
Barclaycard	3,520	UDT	4,000
HFC	2,000	Universal Credit	5,000
Lombard Tricity	1,350	Welbeck	680
Nationwide Anglia	3,600	Yorkshire	3,000

Total unsecured debt: £30,316

Mr and Mrs X, Cleveland			
AA	£3,112	Mercantile Credit	£1,781
Bank of Scotland	1,082	Mercantile Credit	5,542
Barclays	5,357	Midland	1,328
Barclaycard	1,025	UDT	3,018
Barclaycard	1,043	Universal Credit	3,019
Barclaycard	1,384	Welbeck	595
Boston Trust	1,251	Welbeck	642
Citibank	8,121	Yorkshire	561
Comfort Finance	519	Yorkshire	3,986
Comfort Finance	982		

Total unsecured debt: £45,677

Note: Debts on mortgage repayments, fuel, water or telephone bills, or rates are not included.

Source: United Dominions Trust/Citizens Advice Bureaux quoted in 'The future for account sharing systems', by Keith Fowler, paper presented at CCN Systems conference on credit, Guernsey, 1988.

To help to prevent these personal disasters and for lending to become more socially responsible, adjustments must be made in risk assessment systems to take account of the capacity of borrowers to repay loans. In the case of revolving credit (credit cards), for instance, lenders should look at the credit limit *already* extended to a borrower, and how near to this limit the borrower is. This might prevent people from overcommitting themselves on three or more cards, as clearly happened in the examples in the box.

To achieve this, the industry will also need to use information provided by applicants about their income. Almost without exception, consumers expect to be asked for this information. Lenders tell us that they do not make use of income details because they are not a predictor of the probability of repayment and that in any case the information provided on application forms is seldom either comprehensive or accurate.

Yet all the codes of practice of the major sectoral lenders - finance houses, retailers, check traders, door-to-door salesmen, and small moneylenders and collectors - specifically recommend their members to check total indebtedness.

The Finance Houses Association code of practice (July 1987) says, for instance, that a lender should:

> " . . . Where appropriate supply full and accurate information (both positive and negative) to credit reference agencies.
>
> . . . Before granting credit or hire facilities satisfy itself as to the consumer's present and future ability to repay, by taking all reasonable steps, including searching a credit reference agency, to discover the existing commitments of the consumer . . . "

and it continues

> ".... in determining what are reasonable steps and whether a credit reference agency shall be searched, regard may be had to the nature and amount of the facility, the circumstances of the application, and the information provided by the consumer."

These two clauses appear, too, in the codes of practice of the Consumer Credit Trade Association and the National Consumer Credit Federation.

We are reluctant to see further statutory regulation imposed on lenders. But credit agency searches, and the verification and use of information about the borrower's income to assess capacity to repay the loan, are crucial to the prevention of serious consumer overcommitment. We would like to see far higher penalties for lenders who irresponsibly ignore these sections of their codes.

We propose that where loans (or credit limits) of more than £500 are being considered, there should be a statutory duty on the creditor to search agency files. (This is, in fact, a high limit - higher than the average outstanding commitment on credit cards and ten times higher than the banks are prepared to risk on guaranteeing a cheque).

If subsequent default ends in a court case but the lender is unable to prove reasonable care in granting the credit, we recommend that the debt should be unenforceable.

This may have cost implications for those at the lower end of the credit market but the costs of credit agency searches will, we believe, be more than offset by the reduction in bad debts.

4.4 The processing of data

This has been one of the most contentious areas of lending and risk assessment.

The use of 'third party' details - about, for instance, a spouse or lodger, friend or brother, even a former resident at the same address - has been extensively criticised. The Data Protection Registrar has concluded that, while information may have been fairly obtained, it is not being fairly processed. Consequently, to use the data in this way is in breach of the first data protection principle (5).

Sometimes, third party information is simply inaccurate - similar names at the same address, for example, or incorrect spellings. Some lenders use third party information as a predictive variable. Consumers have been particularly enraged when refused credit to discover it was the result of information about someone else. Equally, for one person to receive details of another's credit record is a clear breach of privacy.

By early 1989 the credit industry had offered to negotiate significant changes in the way data was collected and processed. In particular, they indicated they would be prepared to consider:

★ information about the credit record of other people who did not live at the given address at the same time as the applicant would be phased out. In automated risk assessment, this involves designing new scorecards so could not be expected to be completed until the end of 1990;

★ information about people living at the same address at the same time as the applicant, but who are not family members, would also be phased out. This covers circumstances where lodgers contract bad debts, or where property is in multiple occupation such as flats or bedsits. Exactly how this information will be removed is still (early 1990) under discussion. It raises obvious problems of definition (see below).

However, these changes have not yet been made and the industry has resisted dropping the use of information that deals with 'family members' who live at the same address at the same time. Lenders have produced substantive statistical evidence that this information is strongly predictive of risk and is therefore relevant and is used legitimately (6).

Lenders argue too that the removal of every category of third party information would result in a greater number of loan refusals and would increase costs to borrowers. We have no evidence to dispute this, except to point to the experience of other countries where default rates are lower than the UK's without the use of third party information.

However, there are some other developments which we believe would help the industry to phase out third party information more speedily.

4.4.1 MISTAKEN IDENTITIES

Identity checks on applicants and borrowers need to be cast-iron. Names alone are a notorious way of confusing identities. Mistakes are common in, for example, county court judgement forms. John F Smith and John Smith, a father and son who live at the same address, are not unnaturally confused.

A far more accurate double-check on identity is date of birth. Dates of birth are now widely used as fail-safe identifiers, most notably on medical records, and are crucial for large numbers of common surnames - Smith, Jones, Singh, Patel.

Date of birth is not, however, routinely used in credit referencing systems, even though consumers are usually asked to provide it on application forms. Although the Finance Houses Association tells us it is generally pessimistic about the accuracy of the information given on forms, the one fact that *is* typically accurate is the applicant's date of birth. (An interesting variation reported to us is the practice in some US states of issuing a driving licence to *all* their residents on their eighteenth birthday. This acts as an identifier, and is only endorsed as a driving qualification when the appropriate test has been passed.)

The Data Protection Registrar has voiced concern that using dates of birth in credit identity checks could be extended into some form of national identity number. We acknowledge this concern, and obviously any use of date of birth would need to be discussed first with a variety of commercial and government bodies. However, in our view, the potential benefits outweigh the disadvantages. We believe that consumers would have no objection to their birth dates being used in this way, provided they had first given their consent, and that it would be far more acceptable than using other personal identifiers such as National Insurance numbers. It would certainly be more acceptable than the worst examples of mistaken identity and unnecessary refusals of credit.

In Austria, Germany, the USA, and Scandinavia, for example, the use of third party information in credit assessment is either specifically prohibited or is not considered necessary to risk assessment. In some countries this is because there is a national identity number system, others use social security numbers, and others date of birth. Most of these countries, incidentally, have generally had lower interest rates than the United Kingdom over the past ten years. Appendix IV.4 details the regulations in a number of other countries.

4.4.2 INFORMATION ABOUT OTHER MEMBERS OF THE FAMILY

There is a general difficulty about filing "same family" information in credit risk assessment systems, as the Industry Forum itself has acknowledged. How do you identify the *family*? Cohabitation is increasingly common. Married women often keep their maiden name. Adult step-children may be part of the family economic unit.

The National Consumer Council, like many others, is opposed in principle to the use of third party information in credit risk assessment. In Norway, the law prohibits the use of sensitive information on "family affairs other than that referring to family relationships or family status, property arrangements between spouses, and breadwinner status". In addition, third party information may not be used to form "an unjustified or unreasonably negative attitude" about someone (7).

The credit industry in this country argues that data on other members of an applicant's family - however defined - is both strongly predictive of risk and helps to minimise fraud.

We are concerned to strike a balance between the need for responsible credit granting and fair access for consumers at reasonable cost. We are not convinced that "same family" information prevents default; we look to the industry to take up the recommendations we have already made in this section to improve their assessment systems.

Fraud prevention is another matter, and the industry evidence is persuasive. However, we are glad to see new and separate developments in this area, such as the joint Credit Industry Fraud Avoidance System (CIFAS) , and urge the extension of shared initiatives like this as an alternative to the uncertainties, ambiguities and personal intrusions of third party data.

How relevant is a husband's or wife's credit record?

The financial failure of either husband or wife has an impact on the whole family as an "economic unit". This is especially so when there are young children. At the same time, people who live together as a family are individuals with independent rights and often independent means.

In the United States, a lender may not enquire about a spouse or an ex-spouse when an application for credit is *based on the applicant's own income* (except when that income is alimony, child support or another form of maintenance payment from the (ex-) spouse).

Credit-granters in the US *are* required to look at the credit record of any accounts held jointly with a former spouse if the applicant has no credit history of their own. But if the ex-spouse has an unfavourable credit record, the applicant (often non-earning) may show that this does not reflect on his or her own creditworthiness.

In Canada, on the other hand, lenders are allowed to, and do, ask for information about a spouse, especially as regards employment. A credit application is jeopardised if your partner has a poor credit record, although this is not supposed to be the sole consideration.

In both countries, a good independent credit record, before or during marriage, will significantly improve the chance of each partner getting access to more credit.

In this country the market, and risk assessment, are less developed than in north America. Nonetheless, a spouse who is not earning can obtain personal credit on the basis of the earning spouse's income. This, we believe, is an example of third party information used in a positive way.

Where there is evidence of an applicant maintaining an independent credit account in good order, there should be no need to enquire into the record of a spouse or anyone else. But where an applicant has no independent income, it is reasonable to include any available information about the credit history *of a legal spouse* in risk assessment. Applicants should be explicitly told that this may happen when they complete the form.

4.5 Consumer credit data: who should hold the files?

At present, as we have seen, credit referencing is dominated by three large agencies which sell their services to the lending industry. Each compiles its own database. They also share some information, such as that on county court judgements supplied by the Registry Trust, and on suspected and actual fraud.

There was much discussion during the 1980s about the desirability or otherwise of setting up a single national credit register. Indeed much public unease about risk assessment and credit referencing centres on this - the idea of one Big Brother computer system.

Despite this Orwellian fantasy, we believe there would have been major advantages in a single, non-profitmaking institution to hold and safeguard personal credit information and to release that information in a strictly controlled way. This type of large agency exists in other European Community countries - the Credit Registration Bureau (BKR) in Holland, for example, and the Norwegian government-owned Losoreregisterit (public register).

But the moment when such a project might have been feasible in the United Kingdom is past. We must look to the existing system and how it can be adapted to future needs and priorities.

A comprehensive credit database is essential to the prevention of serious personal financial distress and to the credit industry's risk levels. We have already pointed to gaps in the data that is currently compiled and stored. There are even more critical gaps in the way the existing data is circulated.

It is almost inevitable that some data held by one agency will be missing from the records of another. Few lending institutions go to the expense of paying more than one agency. This may mean that borrowers with a variety of debts, registered with different agencies, may not have the true extent of their (over) commitment spotted by the lender.

One solution, given the sophisticated technology of credit referencing, would be to network the databases, allowing for joint information to be supplied to lenders for credit reference purposes only. A proposal like this has obvious implications for competition between the agencies. Nevertheless there are precedents: in the highly competitive United States, the national agencies share information on a coast-to-coast basis.

The basic service offered by credit reference agencies is almost identical. The organisations which supply them with the information on which they depend are also their customers. A bureau can only increase its business by recruiting new customers, and wider information-sharing between bureaux could mean that there would be little to choose from between the existing competitors.

The leading agencies also offer lucrative additional and highly specialised services which many of their customers do choose to buy in. These include scorecard development, staff training, management information systems, debt collection services, geodemographic and marketing information, and access to European information.

So there are real difficulties, in terms of competition policy and the risk of cartel arrangements, in proposing that data be networked. However, we are convinced that credit-granters will move more and more towards sharing *selected* information over the coming ten years, to the benefit of both the industry and its consumers. The changes, for instance, in the powers of public utilities to disconnect consumers may make the privatised industries more interested in risk assessment (especially through performance scoring) and in sharing their data on arrears and default: the sheer volume of data in this event could make networking an attractive proposition.

Such developments would need careful consideration and discussion. To open the debate, we look here at two possible scenarios for wider sharing of information.

Horizontal networking

This would involve sharing information *across* lending institutions and credit reference agencies. The information might be restricted to default data (including that from the public utilities), or widened to credit account data as well. Access would be limited to licensed lenders only, with new and rigorous codes of practice to regulate the use made of the information.

It would be possible to exclude from this pool "white" information on credit accounts (see section 4.2.1) so that credit reference agencies would still be in a position to compete in this area and lenders to contract in to the variety of other services that agencies offer individually. The value and implications of this would need to be carefully thought out.

Vertical integration

This would mean a radical restructuring within the credit reference business. It would involve the isolation of, for example, all credit reference data - with a single access point for all licensed lenders and agencies.

One way to achieve this would be for the three largest credit reference agencies, the Registry Trust and other public bodies to set up a holding company to administer the single networked database. Such a body should also have consumer representation.

We believe the Parliamentary Under-Secretary of State for Industry and Consumer Affairs already has powers over the operation and regulation of credit reference agencies, under section 26 of the Consumer Credit Act 1974. Tighter controls would not necessarily, therefore, need primary legislation.

Either of these methods of information-sharing - horizontal or vertical - would bring major benefits from a consumer point of view. They would give an identifiable source for subject access to credit records and for complaints or for registering a correction. With a corporate identity, visible accountability and strict controls, such a system would be far more reassuring to consumers than the existing piecemeal and largely invisible operations.

But we recognise that the data-providers will need convincing that information-sharing is in their own best interests. This will mean consultation and negotiation, through a multi-sector forum. The National Consumer Council would be happy to contribute to this.

In addition, improvements are needed in the "visibility" of credit reference agencies. In other words, consumers must be made more aware of the existence and value of agencies, and have greater confidence in them to keep personal data securely.

4.6 The consumer interest in credit referencing

4.6.1 CONSUMER ATTITUDES

In a paper on the commercial use of financial information in 1988 (8), we reported that consumers were divided - for and against - the use of credit reference agencies.

This somewhat contradictory finding also emerged in the PAS Office of Fair Trading's 1987 survey (9). Over two in three respondents thought that credit reference agencies were a good idea. Approval decreased with age, perhaps reflecting some suspicion among older people unfamiliar with, and nervous of, new technology. People who used credit were marginally more likely to be in favour, while those who did not use credit seemed more worried about possible invasions of privacy.

Half the respondents felt that a credit reference agency protected or prevented consumers from overspending or getting into debt. Just under one in three acknowledged that lenders needed to assess whether or not an applicant was a good credit risk.

At the same time nearly half *also* thought that the agencies were an invasion of privacy - "they should mind their own business". There was a high level of mistrust about incorrect information going on files without the individual's knowledge. Despite these suspicions, only 2 per cent of the sample had ever tried to find out what information was held about them on credit reference agency files.

It is clear from this evidence that the credit and credit reference industries need to address the problem of confused and ambivalent attitudes among consumers with some urgency. Without consumer confidence in risk assessment systems, little progress is likely to be made in improving them.

Here we look at some specific worries and at how other countries have tackled some of the issues involved.

4.6.2 INFORMATION, ACCURACY AND DISCLOSURE

Consumers have serious anxieties about the confidentiality of information held about them, about its accuracy and about how it is used. We are of the view that systems that store and use personal information should be highly visible - not in terms of the commercial calculations used by lenders to assess risks, but in terms of accuracy and consumer access.

In the United States, Sweden and Norway, data subjects are fully informed of requests to see their files. In Sweden and Norway, when the information is disclosed to a lender, an identical copy must go to the person it is about, free of charge.

Whenever a data subject - the consumer - files a correction, the agency holding the data must send the corrected file to every organisation that has received a copy of the original over the previous twelve months. In Norway this will be done almost automatically because agencies there can be sued for passing on inaccurate information and therefore have an obligation to correct.

Quite apart from the virtue of all this in informing consumers what is recorded about them, it makes them aware of the benefits of a good credit record. They become familiar with the kind of data that is used and how it is presented. They also get to know who is storing information about them *and* to whom it is being released, and for what purpose.

Consumers are reassured that the data makes no judgements, simply records facts, and if those facts are wrong, either accidentally or involving fraud, there is an immediate early warning that helps both the consumer and the lender.

We strongly commend these safeguards. We would like to see them become a standard of good practice among lenders and have them included in UK data protection legislation. There are, however, large cost implications, as well as extra staff burdens, in such proposals. While we firmly believe the principle to be sound, we acknowledge that the size of the UK credit industry and the widespread use of credit militate against putting it fully into practice. We should like to explore a solution acceptable to lenders, agencies and, above all, borrowers themselves. In France, for example, a credit refusal obliges the lender to send a copy of any file to the applicant.

4.6.3 CONFIRMATION OF IDENTITY

We have seen (in section 4.4) that the existing identity check systems are a minefield, from the point of view both of getting identity wrong and of wrongly disclosing personal information to a third party.

One major problem has been the way data is processed, searching by *address* rather than name, and we welcome the industry's promise to develop software that will search by *name and address* and will also link current with past addresses. An even more reliable method, as we have said, would be to add *date of birth* to identity searches.

Consumers also need to be made more aware of the importance of giving full, unambiguous information about their names, both past and present. This has been a special problem on county court judgement forms and we welcome the steps the Registry Trust is taking to tighten up.

Another real difficulty is that credit reference services rely heavily on the electoral register, as we have seen. A small minority of people choose not to be on the electoral register. Their credit opportunities should not, we believe, be written off through this decision. We should like to see a "confirm identity" flag attached to these applications, so that the applicant can be asked to provide extra proof of identity.

4.6.4 CONSENT AND 'FAIR OBTAINING'

Should lenders and credit reference agencies be obliged to get a consumer's express consent to filing and releasing personal financial information?

We have examined what happens in some other countries.

In Norway, there do not appear to be any rules specifically about informed consent. It is up to the applicant to decide whether or not to disclose information, and up to the lender to decide whether or not to make the loan, and on what terms. However, how the information is used, stored and subsequently disclosed is strictly controlled.

In Sweden, the Credit Information Act does not give data subjects a right of prior consent nor a veto over the release of records that may form part of a credit assessment. They do, however, have the safeguard of being sent a copy of their file at the time of disclosure (see section 4.6.2).

In the United States, borrowers are deemed to have waived their right to informed consent in return for the opportunity to get credit.

The law in the United Kingdom is less specific. But in 1988 the Data Protection Registrar said that under the principle of fair obtaining of information, consumers should consent to disclosure. They should be told the purpose for which they are being asked for information, where it will be filed, who else will see it, and other ways in which it might be used. Some lenders have begun to put notification clauses along these lines in their application forms.

Also in 1988 the Jack Committee on Banking Services (10) recommended that bank customers should be asked for express consent to disclosure to third parties. "Express consent" means consent in writing, with a statement of the purpose for which consent has been given.

There is a difficulty here, however. To comply with the Data Protection Registrar's guidance, an applicant for credit must not be unduly pressured into disclosing information. A refusal to lend *except subject to consent to disclosure* is, in the Registrar's view, equivalent to undue duress - and therefore amounts to "unfair obtaining".

We have considered the various options carefully, and have come to the view that it is sufficient, reasonable, and in the long-term interests of consumers for lenders to inform applicants that information will be lodged with a credit reference agency and to tell them how it will be used.

Combined with the safeguards we have already discussed, this would not, we feel, amount to undue duress. Consumers make a free decision to apply for credit, the terms of which are subject to other joint obligations. Provided all the obligations are specifically recognised by both parties, this information clause would be a reasonable part of the contract - and one that will be important after the phasing-out of third party information in assessment systems.

The Jack Committee also recommended that where there had been a breakdown in the banker-customer relationship arising out of default by the customer, the requirement for express consent to passing on personal information should be waived. This enables the bank to file information on defaulting customers with a credit reference agency. Similar provisos are made in other countries and it is one that we support.

In section 5.2 we make firm recommendations about many of the points on risk assessment techniques discussed in this section.

References to section 4

1. Andrew H. Pople and Mark J. Smith, *Who Wants A National Credit Register?* (the black and white debate), City University Business School, 1988 (draft)
2. Janet Ford, *The Indebted Society: credit and default in the 1980s*, Routledge, 1988; Clare Ungerson and John Baldock, *Rent Arrears in Ashford*, Department of Social Administration and Social Work, University of Kent, Canterbury, 1978.
3. National Consumer Council, *Security Risks: personal loans secured on homes*, NCC, 1987.
4. Office of Fair Trading, *Overindebtedness: a report by the Director General of Fair Trading*, July 1989.
5. Data Protection Registrar, *Credit and the Assessment of Individuals: response to the report "Striking the balance - the way ahead" which has been prepared by the (Credit) Industry Forum on Data Protection*, E.J. Howe, February 1989; Guideline 4: Data Protection Act 1984, *The Data Protection Principles*, February 1989.
6. Industry on Data Protection, *"Striking the Balance": the way ahead*, response to the Data Protection Registrar's concerns about the supply and use of address based "other name" and "similar name and address" information, part II, November 1988.
7. *Norway Act number 48*, 9 June 1978, chapter 3, section 6.
8. National Consumer Council, *Taking Liberties: Commercial use of personal financial information*, NCC, July 1988, PD16/88.
9. PAS Business Surveys, *Consumers' Use of Credit Survey*, for the Office of Fair Trading, 1987.
10. *Banking Services: law and practice*, report by the Review Committee, HMSO, 1989, Cm. 622, (Chairman: Professor R.B. Jack, CBE).

5. Our recommendations

Credit is a very popular consumer product. In the ten years since our last major report on the subject, as this review has shown, supply has boomed, new ways of delivering the product have been developed, and most consumers have readier access to an ever-widening range of loans. This is all to the good.

Our book has also charted some of the serious problems these dramatic changes have brought for some individuals, and touched on some potential problems for society at large. Our Introduction reviewed these tension areas in the supply and use of credit and raised some broad questions that in our view need to be addressed in the 1990s.

In this final section, we turn to some of the specific issues of consumer concern that have appeared throughout our review, and suggest some points for action.

The problems of detail that we highlight here, and therefore our remedies, share a common thread. It is in the nature of lending money that a proportion of loans will not be repaid. It is in the nature of borrowing that a proportion of borrowers will take on too much credit in relation to their existing income or that their income will plummet suddenly and unexpectedly after taking on what seemed to be reasonable commitments.

In the 1980s, the combined effect of fiscal, demographic and market trends was to push some of these proportions to unacceptable levels. Many consumers have been granted loans of a size and of a kind to turn domestic finances into a nightmare. We foresee some forms of credit multiplying these household disasters even further in the 1990s.

Our recommendations in this section are therefore largely targeted at reducing the ravages brought about by overcommitment, default and insolvency - but in ways that do not undermine prudent, competitive credit-granting on the one hand, nor reasonable access, choice and value-for-money for consumers on the other.

5.1 Consumer information and advice about credit

Clear, comprehensive and straightforward information is essential to consumers when they are choosing whether, and what, to buy.

5.1.1 CREDIT ADVERTISING AND PROMOTION

We warmly welcome the safeguards introduced in 1988 and 1989 into the regulations governing advertisements for, and information about, secured loans for purchases other than property, following our 1987 report *Security Risks*. Borrowers now have to be openly warned that their home is at stake if they miss repayments.

We remain uneasy about some other advertising for consumer loans. Claims that you can have "instant" and "easy" access could be understood by consumers to mean that no credit checks are carried out and to contribute to an impression - largely a false one - of carelessness in lending. Advertisements that offer loans for holidays and luxury household goods without giving equal emphasis to the fact that the loan will be secured against your home are, in our view, irresponsible.

People who are short of money or who are financially unsophisticated are vulnerable. We should like to see more scrupulous and universal adherence to the *British Code of Advertising Practice* guideline that says:

> "No advertiser should seek to take improper advantage of any characteristic or circumstance which may make consumers vulnerable; as, for example, by exploiting their credulity or their lack of experience or knowledge in any manner detrimental to their interests." (1)

Some promotional techniques are similarly questionable, in particular aggressive selling of credit in shops and department stores. Credit accounts promoted through special offers, through in-store "personality girls", or through commission to staff who recruit new account customers all raise questions about how credit should be marketed. It is our view that these kinds of techniques encourage impulse-buying and overcommitment and that they often imply low lending standards.

We repeat our view that borrowers need to be fully informed and explicitly reminded about the seriousness of credit transactions and the consequences of overcommitting their household budgets. It might be too much to expect lending institutions to make this explicit in their advertising. But there are opportunities at the point of sale, in particular on credit application forms. The form might, for instance, include a blank income and expenditure sheet which consumers could fill in *if they wished*, as a way of reminding them that what they are signing will have consequences in the way of repayment obligations. *We urge lending institutions to consider these and other ways of bringing home to applicants the serious nature of a credit commitment.*

5.1.2 MONEY ADVICE

The whole area of independent advice to debtors merits a book to itself. We can only briefly touch on it here, and refer readers to recently published reports (2 and 3) for more detailed studies. (And see *A Report on Debt Advice Provision in the UK*, National Consumer Council, forthcoming.)

Helping to prevent people from getting into debt is an enormous task, as this review has perhaps shown. Trying to help people out of a financial mess and back into normal life is equally difficult.

Unmanageable debt is still, by and large, a secret that most families are ashamed of, and are certainly reluctant to share. It causes different problems for different kinds of household - single parents, young low-income families, the unemployed, the elderly. The skills required to understand and unravel the web of what may be years of financial muddle, and then work out a reasonable solution, are in short supply.

However, a small but growing army of "money advisers" and "debt counsellors" has grown up over the decade. These are thinly scattered. And they range from independent agencies acting wholly in consumers' interests to advisers whose first concern is the creditor.

Independent and semi-independent advisers:
citizens advice bureaux (CABx)
consumer protection/trading standards departments
Department of Social Security - special case officers
members of the Federation of Independent Advice Centres (FIAC)
housing aid centres
legal advice centres
social work departments and probation service
charities, such as the SSAFA (Soldiers', Sailors' and Airmen's Families Association)

Creditor-based advisers:
banks
building societies
finance houses
fuel boards
local-authority based, such as housing officers
retail lenders (especially store credit card operators)
other lenders

Creditor-based advisers, often working against difficult odds, can be an important source of advice. They may give borrowers a breathing space in which to reorganise their budgets. However, they rarely get the full picture of one family's commitment, and of course they are *not* independent. Usually they are employed principally to recover the money owing to them, not to help the debtor to re-schedule all his debts according to personal priority.

An important source of independent money advice services is the voluntary sector. About 300 advisers are sited in citizens' advice bureaux. Four voluntary Money Advice Centres provide casework services and eighteen Money Advice "Support Units" give specialist back-up services to and through the most accessible local agencies, via consultancy, training and some specialist casework. There is also a Housing Debtline, which provides telephone advice and information to anyone in the UK, and is based at Birmingham Settlement.

Nonetheless, there are still comparatively few centres with specially trained, multi-disciplinary advisers. Those there are find their services much in demand, to the extent that the staff can be overwhelmed by the volume of enquiries. Indeed, independent money advisers are forced to keep a fairly low profile, simply in order to cope with their existing workload.

In 1982 we identified only sixteen specialist money advice services in Britain, and argued strongly for their expansion (4). There has been some response, but mainly from the already stretched voluntary sector. The latest survey of debt advice provision (5) shows that there are 290 (equivalent to) full-time debt advice workers in the UK and almost 290 part-time unpaid workers - volunteers - who contribute about 16 per cent of the total service.

Extrapolating from this, we calculate that in 1987 the ratio of money plaints heard in the county courts to independent money advice workers would have been nearly 8,000 to 1. From the Office of Fair Trading projections of borrowers with repayment difficulties (6), there are potentially over 15,000 clients for each independent debt adviser. Of course, not everyone will want, or eventually need, to go to a money adviser. But the OFT survey also shows that many borrowers in difficulty had nowhere to turn for independent advice. This implies that many multiple debtors are still muddling along in financial chaos, without any outside help. Urgent improvements are needed in the provision and availability of independent money advice.

The problem is funding. In 1989 this amounted to nearly £1.4 million for England and Wales. Over half of this came from local authorities, and a fifth from urban and community programme funds. The private sector

Sources of funding for all money advice initiatives in England and Wales (5)

Type of funder	£	%
local authorities	709,845	50
urban programme	275,443	19
NACAB/local authority	102,995	7
community programme	12,800	1
charitable trusts	56,370	4
private sector	230,000	16
other	40,150	3
	£1,427,603	100

contributed 16 per cent (£230,000). Some of the major creditors supply very little in the way of funds for independent consumer advice - the fuel and water boards, for example.

Ways and means of funding money advice services has been the subject of a joint Finance Houses Association and Money Advice working party. They have examined a variety of models, for example, a money advice services trust; a charitable foundation; or a trust linked to a sponsorship broker who would work directly with credit companies. Others have suggested that lenders put up an individual bond, which could be drawn upon as and when the lender is involved in a debt advice case. Those lenders with high bad debt ratios would contribute proportionately more than those with good credit portfolios. *We welcome all these proposals and look forward to seeing them tested in practice.*

Other funding options could be considered.

Under Consumer Credit Act legislation, lenders have to be licensed. For this they pay a fee, of around £150 plus an extra £10 for each additional licence category (such as debt collector, credit reference agency, and so on). This is an exceptionally modest charge. As we have pointed out elsewhere (7), businesses registering with self regulatory organisations under the Financial Services Act have to pay between £700 and £1,200 for membership (in this case, of FIMBRA). At the upper end of the range, fees are over £15,000.

We recommend that the Department of Trade and Industry review the licence fees for consumer credit and ancillary businesses. There is, we believe, a strong case for looking at a new system of graded-fee licences, under the consumer credit legislation, according to the turnover value of the business.

At present, the money from licences goes directly to the Treasury, rather than being fed back into the costs of regulating and monitoring lenders and their associated businesses. *We should like to see a major part of this money diverted directly to money advice services, to be negotiated by the Department of Trade and Industry and the Office of Fair Trading.*

There have been other, more sweeping recommendations - such as a consumer credit levy. This has often been proposed in the context of a brake on consumer spending, but it could also act as a funding source for money advice services. While this has wider economic implications, it is important to recognise that many of the precipitating factors to unmanageable commitment are *outside* the individual control of either the borrower or the industry. Unemployment rates are a typical example. The stock market crash of October 1987 similarly had unforeseen effects on both lenders and borrowers. There are also the effects of interest rate "hikes", which form a crucial plank of current monetary policy. Borrowers who are heavily committed find it almost impossible to increase their level of repayments at short notice, and this may lead to increased levels of default. Girobank, for example, increased their bad debt provision for 1989 from

£5.7 million to £11.9 million "because of the impact of high interest rates on personal lending", according to a press report (8).

It is the volatility of such external factors that makes it very difficult for borrowers to keep a tight control on their commitments once they have taken them on. This is particularly worrying given the trend of the industry to "lend large and lend long", when macroeconomic factors are likely to play an important, and unpredictable, role in debt repayments. Long-term funding of money advice services therefore cannot be the responsibility of local government and the credit industry alone. *It is an absolute priority that secure long-term funding is provided for money advice services through the Department of Trade and Industry and the Lord Chancellor's Department.*

A further aspect of money advice services - the potential for closer links with the embryonic British credit union movement - is discussed in section 5.6.1.

5.2 Risk assessment and credit referencing

Credit is a lifeline to millions of borrowers, helping some families through lean times and improving the quality of life for others. The development of manual and, more especially, automated credit risk assessment has helped larger numbers of people to get credit quickly and more efficiently, and has played a part in holding down levels of default.

At the same time, the systems are still developing. They need refining - to play a more active role in spotting the early, obvious signs of borrowers running into financial straits and to achieve a better balance between the need to look thoroughly into an applicant's credentials for a loan and the need to safeguard personal privacy and confidentiality. Our recommendations aim to steer that middle course.

5.2.1 CREDIT REFERENCING DATA: THIRD PARTY INFORMATION

In section 4, we discussed the use of "third party" information in credit reference systems. We accept the lenders' evidence that checks on people other than the applicant help to reduce fraud and to distinguish between good and bad credit risks. A ban on the use of third party information might initially reduce the number of people granted credit while lenders raise their risk margins. It would also involve the design of new scoring systems and would therefore probably mean a change-over period. Nevertheless, we strongly believe that all the interested parties should work towards a system in which the principles of confidentiality and fair processing of information take precedence.

We recommend that lenders and credit reference agencies phase out the use of "third party" information in credit risk assessment as a matter of urgency. The only circumstance, we believe, in which such information could fairly be used is in the assessment of a non-earning legal spouse who has no credit record of their own.

5.2.2 BETTER INFORMATION, AND MORE OF IT

Our recommendations here are primarily addressed to the lending institutions - the Finance Houses Association, the Council of Mortgage Lenders, and banks - and the credit reference agencies.

To reduce cases of mistaken identity and lower the risk of personal information being disclosed to the wrong person, *we urge lending institutions and credit reference agencies to explore with the Home Office the use of date of birth along with name and address in identity check systems.*

The information currently compiled by agencies as a basis for checking creditworthiness has serious gaps. In section 4, we offered a list of the categories of data that need adding to consumer databases to make them more comprehensive and therefore more effective. One of these categories needs including on files as a matter of urgency.

We recommend that all the institutions making secured loans should supply information on serious mortgage arrears and default on secured loans to credit reference agencies. This would be used for risk assessment purposes.

To improve risk assessment and debt prevention still further, *we recommend that the public utilities, other creditors and credit reference agencies explore systems for sharing information on default on electricity, gas and water accounts.* This information should only be disclosed after notification to the consumer in default.

Risk assessment currently relies too heavily on evidence of a borrower repaying loans, however small and over however long a period, and not enough on an applicant's total current commitments. This emphasis reflects the industry's interest in increasing people's use of credit, but does little to safeguard consumers tempted into overcommitment. *We recommend that lenders take into account an applicant's income plus any available information on his or her other commitments, especially the use of credit limits on credit cards, before approving a loan and when monitoring the performance of a credit account.*

An additional method of checking multiple indebtedness - and reducing outright fraud - is already available, but is not used. On a credit reference agency search, the lender is told how many others have searched that file previously, but not whether they granted credit. *We recommend that lenders register when a loan has been granted following a search.*

5.2.3 WIDER USE OF RISK ASSESSMENT

As we have seen, the credit industry is not universally scrupulous in following the recommendations of its own codes of practice when it comes to using risk assessment systems and checking an applicant's total commitments. *We recommend that the Department of Trade and Industry amend the Consumer Credit Act 1974 to place a duty on lenders to make a credit reference search for all loans or revolving credit limits of £500 or more.*

For loans of more than £500, if a debtor is subsequently brought to court for non-payment, the lender should, we believe, have to show that it took all reasonable care in granting the loan, including consulting a credit reference agency. *In line with the recommendation above, the Department of Trade and Industry should amend the Consumer Credit Act, so that if a lender cannot prove that a careful check was made, the debt should be treated as unenforceable.*

Both these two recommendations would require primary legislation to give additional strength to the Consumer Credit Act 1974.

5.2.4 SHARING INFORMATION

Commercial confidentiality is important to lenders. So is more reliable risk assessment. We believe the industry's access to comprehensive credit referencing information needs to be as wide as possible. *We recommend to the lending institutions, public utility creditors and the credit reference agencies that they set up a joint consortium to explore ways of exchanging and updating credit reference information.*

In section 4 we proposed some networking options as a means of wider information-sharing. Any networking of databases must have the confidence not only of the industry but also of its consumers. Credit referencing systems generally lack public visibility and accountability. *We would welcome any improvements made by credit reference services to explain their operations and functions to consumers*

5.2.5 CONSUMER PROTECTION AND INFORMATION

It is a reasonable component of a loan transaction that information about the borrower is filed with a credit reference agency, so long as the borrower is explicitly informed about this. However, this requires some specific extra safeguards (already adopted in some other countries: see section 4.6.2).

We recommend that lending institutions and others using credit reference agencies revise their application forms to improve the transparency of the risk assessment administrative system.

When information is lodged with an agency, consumers should be notified and told their rights of access to the file under section 158 of the Consumer Credit Act 1974 and under the Data Protection Act 1984.

We also recommend that lending institutions, retailers and credit reference agencies explore ways of keeping their borrowers informed of the information held about them. In principle, we should prefer a system through which any lender asking for information on an individual would send a copy of their file to the data subject, free of charge. Since this is likely to have substantial cost implications, a compromise satisfactory to all the interested parties may be necessary. The National Consumer Council would be happy to participate in discussions on this.

However, where an amendment about a data subject is subsequently filed, all lenders who have previously searched the file should be notified by the agency holding the file.

It would be helpful to consumers to have a single access point for the information held on them by the agencies and to have confidence that any corrections to their files will be registered by all the major agencies. *We recommend that the major credit reference agencies explore ways of sharing the costs of 'subject access requests', perhaps involving lenders, so as to achieve economies of scale and to improve consumer confidence in their operation.*

5.3 Credit insurance

No risk assessment system will ever be infallible. Some consumers who would have repaid regularly and conscientiously will be refused credit, and in section 5.2 our recommendations tackle some aspects of this problem.

Others will be granted credit and, for some of the huge variety of reasons we have discussed, will then be unable to repay it.

Consumer use of credit insurance is growing, but very slowly. There are still too many cases where insurance would have saved a borrower who suddenly falls ill, for example, or becomes unemployed. The 1989 Office of Fair Trading report on indebtedness estimated that around 1.5 million borrowers had had difficulties with repayment through unemployment.

A crucial aspect of the low take-up of insurance is the way in which borrowers assess their need for it. When the National Consumer Council was drawing up policy recommendations for our 1980 report *Consumers and Credit*, we examined - but rejected - the option of mandatory insurance. Instead, we urged lenders to persuade customers to take it out voluntarily and, because insurance is such a valuable consumer protection, we proposed that lenders make it a 'negative option' in credit applications - that is, that the applicant has to make a deliberate choice not to buy the insurance.

However, as insurance schemes have become more common, especially for revolving credit, consumers have shown some resistance to a method that smacks of inertia selling. People who do not want insurance are aggrieved when they subsequently discover they have been paying for it. They are also put to the inconvenience and expense of cancelling the policy.

In the direct marketing industry, responsible companies are gradually reversing the practice of passing on names and addresses for marketing purposes without permission. This is not only excellent from the consumers' point of view, it apparently pays dividends for direct marketing businesses: there is evidence that people are prepared to give *more* information once they have been asked for their informed consent and that direct marketing is subsequently better received (9). It follows that more research is needed in this area, and specifically into how consumers perceive information about credit insurance.

Research shows that people discount the risks when specifically advised to take out insurance. The Finance Houses Association has found that only 10 per cent of borrowers took it out on an "opt-in", positive clause and still only 30 per cent on an "opt-out", negative clause (although, more cheeringly, only one in ten of the second group subsequently decided to cancel).

New ways of inducing borrowers to protect themselves and to adjust their "it won't happen to me" attitude need to be explored. This is a responsibility for both the lending industry and for those representing consumer interests, and we hope to see joint discussions.

An obvious starting point is at the point of sale, where borrowers need clear and specific information, given by trained staff. Since consumers who take out insurance are increasing their own costs while the lender is reducing its risk margin, we are strongly opposed to commissions for staff insurance sales. There may be scope, however, for better terms to be offered to customers who do opt for insurance cover (- a scheme that would, of course, require strict safeguards).

Meanwhile, consumers should be able to make a free and informed choice, based on clear information, about whether to take credit insurance or not. *The credit industry and others should discontinue using 'negative options' on credit application forms. Should they continue with the practice, we recommend that the Department of Trade and Industry introduce appropriate legislation.*

5.4 Revolving credit

Consumers find credit and store cards a flexible and convenient way of paying for goods and services. The rise in credit card use in the ten years since *Consumers and Credit* has been substantial.

At the same time, more people have repayment difficulties with credit cards than with other forms of credit. The figures are sufficiently worrying to lead us to look for new safeguards, particularly for those consumers using credit cards for essentials, as opposed to optional or luxury items. A large number of young adults (eighteen to twenty-four year olds) and a smaller - but still significant - number of twenty-five to thirty-four year olds have more problems with credit cards than other types of loan.

5.4.1 CAPACITY TO REPAY

The age ranges give us some clues about the kind of safeguards that are needed. Teenagers and young adults tend to be highly mobile - geographically, socially and financially. Their circumstances change rapidly - from school, perhaps through college or university, to paid employment, or other occupation. They acquire partners and children. Many become home owners for the first time.

Stability of repayment is likely to be a particularly unsound basis for deciding whether or not to make a loan to consumers at this stage of their lives, not only because the youngest of them will have more or less blank credit records but also because of the rapidly changing circumstances of all under-thirty-fives.

Furthermore, good channels of communication between lenders and borrowers are essential. Lenders need to know about an applicant's income and other commitments *before* granting credit and then to assess these regularly once a loan has been made, for instance by evaluating how borrowers use their full credit limit.

We therefore repeat the proposals we made in section 4 - that *the criteria by which lenders assess an applicant's creditworthiness need to steer less towards repayment stability and more towards the person's capacity to take on a new commitment or to service an existing one. We recommend that lenders and credit reference agencies explore ways of incorporating income into automated credit scoring systems.*

5.4.2 CREDIT LIMITS

Another feature of revolving credit that causes anxiety is the practice of raising credit limits automatically, without reference to the customer. The majority of respondents in the Office of Fair Trading's 1987 survey (10) believed that the level of credit granted should be linked to a person's income, and that credit card limits should only be raised at the customer's request. (Indeed, some newer credit cards are specifically promoted on this basis.) *We recommend to the banks, retail lenders and other credit institutions that no limit on a credit card should be increased unless the customer expressly asks for it.*

5.4.3 CREDIT CARD CHARGES

This brings us on to the costs of revolving credit - both the charges for supplying them and the amounts that users repay each month. Our recommendations here are addressed to all credit card providers - the banks, retail lenders and other creditors.

Many heavy credit card users maintain a stable repayment record by making only minimum monthly repayments. Eventually, of course, some of them borrow up to their full credit limit with only a slim chance of ever being able to clear the debt. And some of these borrow even more in an attempt to reduce their debts - sometimes successfully, sometimes disastrously.

Together with other evidence about how consumers assess the costs of credit, this points to the conclusion that many borrowers are more sensitive to *monthly* rates of repayment than to total cost. This has implications for the way credit card suppliers charge their customers.

The monthly repayments charged on credit cards are currently a proportion of the money borrowed so far. *If the monthly repayment were increased proportionately according to the borrower's credit limit, as well as to the balance owing each month, this would alert the borrower to the possibility of overcommitment, and we so recommend.* Since the amount of the monthly repayment is set as part of the individual banks' 'Terms and Conditions of Use', this recommendation would not require legislation.

At the very least, this system of charging would minimise the chances of a very rapid build-up of interest due on repeated use of the card, and would certainly bring a closer relationship between higher credit limits and higher capacity to repay.

The second aspect of charging that concerns us is the comparatively high rates of interest, compounded by the cross-subsidy paid by credit card users to "free riders" (those who pay off their monthly bills each month and incur no interest). It is curious, it seems to us, that consumers who pay for their extended credit get no additional services. A strong candidate for one extra service is fuller information.

We recommend that credit card users should receive a quarterly or six-monthly full statement about their account. This service should be free of charge to interest-payers; "free riders" should be able to elect to have it, for a fee, if they wish.

This statement could show, for instance:

★ the total purchases made in the period
★ the total cash price of those purchases
★ the total interest charges paid
★ the current balance owed
★ the current credit limit and the minimum repayment
★ the current APR, and the previous one if it has changed
★ the credit insurance charge

With this statement, we should like to see a reassessment form attached for the customer to fill in at least six-monthly - along the lines of *Have your circumstances and needs changed?*

The same service could of course be offered to free riders, at a fee: this might be popular among people who use their cards for tax-deductible and other non-personal purposes.

5.5 Secured lending

In our earlier chapters, we have expressed grave concern about the trend towards secured lending for short-term needs and luxury purchases and the growing market in equity release schemes. These trends raise many important wider economic questions, and we reiterate our anxiety here.

It cannot be in the interests of the credit industry to concentrate their lending in a sector so closely dependent on external forces. Small shifts in property prices, in unemployment or in inflation figures can have acute prudential effects. For consumers, such changes can mean more default and repossessions and, if risk margins are raised, reduced access to credit.

We believe the problems that could follow over-enthusiastic secured lending need to be addressed urgently.

We have noted the trend towards "lending large and lending long". This trend is likely to continue and borrowers (especially of secured loans) are therefore increasingly likely to borrow sums that are outside the protection of the Consumer Credit Act - that is, loans for more than £15,000. *We therefore recommend that the Department of Trade and Industry increase the upper limit for loans that fall within the scope of the Consumer Credit Act to £25,000.*

In the past we have highlighted the irresponsibility of some brokers in arranging secured loans for borrowers who have little or no hope of repaying. We make recommendations on this in section 5.7.

A secured loan *can* offer a borrower a good bargain. Consumers can only assess whether or not this is so on the basis of full information about credit costs. *We recommend that the Director General of Fair Trading issues regular guidance on prevailing interest rates for different types of loans. These should be widely publicised.*

5.6 Low-income borrowers: some ways forward

5.6.1 MONEY MANAGEMENT AND CREDIT UNIONS

While credit unions can offer significant help to disadvantaged borrowers, they are *not* a panacea for all credit ills. Recent studies (11) show that those on low incomes welcomed the opportunity to make small regular savings, just as much as to gain access to low-interest credit. Where community credit unions are concerned, there are often substantial spin-offs - greater neighbourhood involvement, literacy schemes, self-help cooperatives, and funding of new community services (launderettes or clubs)

Credit unions, particularly the community-based ones, are under-funded and under-resourced. We especially see the potential for closer links with colleagues in the debt counselling and money advice field. The small savings promoted by community credit unions offer a safe environment for debtors to recover a measure of self-respect and control over their own finances.

Community credit unions would benefit greatly from the development of some sort of funding initiative - perhaps a charity or trust fund, to provide "seed" money for new community unions, as well as funds for training and resource material. We understand there are some initiatives examining the merits of such a scheme and believe there is considerable scope for more development work in this area. *We recommend that the National Federation of Credit Unions and the Association of British Credit Unions Ltd jointly explore cost-effective ways of providing training and other resources for community credit unions.*

5.6.2 THE SOCIAL FUND

The social fund - as currently constituted - is no solution to the borrowing needs of very low-income households. Grants based on entitlement have been replaced by discretionary loans, with no significant increase in the standard benefits. The incomes of some families are too low to be considered even for these loans - the "poverty disqualification". Where do these applicants turn for help? Often the only source is the high-interest, commercial moneylender, pushing the family further into the vicious circle of intractable debt.

At the same time, a social fund represents, in principle, the germ of a good idea. So-called "social loans" and social lending institutions have long been in operation in the rest of Europe. In France, Credit Municipal has a three-hundred year tradition of serving people on low incomes. Originally founded as a monopoly pawnbroking service, it now offers short and medium-term credit to over one million customers, accounting for 10 per cent of the personal credit market in France. Credit Municipal has moved from traditional pawnbroking to providing small loans to poorer borrowers. It will also take on consolidation loans, of particular value where people have become entangled with multiple debts.

In Holland, there are similar institutions - the municipal credit banks - set up as part of a drive against usury. Lending money to the poorest members of society, they were required to operate on a cost-covering basis only, taking over the role of social and charitable lending organisations. Since the commercial banks entered the consumer credit field in the late 1950s, municipal credit banks have declined in importance. However, there are still 49 in operation, and their services are available to nearly all Dutch citizens.

In 1982 the Dutch government decided that public assistance money should not be used to cover debt repayments. Instead, the municipal credit banks were given authority by the government to meet the borrowing needs of the poorest members of society, as well as consolidating and rescheduling existing debts, and providing debt counselling. The rationale was that:

> "... people on welfare, ex-prisoners, foreign workers, divorced women ... won't find it easy to get loans from commercial banks. As it is undesirable for such people to be barred from credit facilities altogether, it is a good thing to have institutions in the margin of the market which serve these disadvantaged citizens on responsible terms." (12)

We have outlined the French and Dutch social lending schemes because we believe they fill a specific and very important gap in a country's credit market. This is the gap that the UK social fund was set up to bridge but, we believe, is failing to do. In many ways, the further development of credit unions could fulfil part of this role. However, they are not suited to meet the emergency needs of people whose budgets are too fully committed to have any possibility of putting money aside for savings. There is wide scope for a truly independent, social lending institution in this country. *We should like to see coordinated research to take this a stage further, exploring the potential for expanding the role of existing financial institutions, and developing new ones.*

5.7 Creditors' default procedures

As some lending institutions are starting to recognise, the way they treat those borrowers who do run into financial difficulties can make those difficulties better, or worse, and can affect the chances of repayment.

Default processes are traditionally based on the notion that a defaulting borrower is wilfully withholding repayment. Of course this is sometimes true. But as we have seen, the reasons why a household gets into debt and a borrower's capacity to repay his or her commitments are often far less controllable.

The big stick of threats or summonses is notoriously counter-productive when a borrower is simply unable to repay. Fuel boards can be particularly aggressive, for instance, in pursuing arrears on credit sale agreements for items like household electrical appliances. They can, and do, insist on installing prepayment meters to collect both the credit sale debt *and* the fuel consumption payments, with the threat of disconnection for any further arrears. It is a form of preferential debt consolidation and collection that can push a consumer who was just managing the budget into unmanageable and disastrous debt. *We recommend that this practice should be disallowed, under the licensing provisions of the relevant Acts.*

Others - notably some finance brokers - exhibit wholly irresponsible methods by sending out a default notice one week and an offer of further credit the next. This ranges from offers of consolidation loans, through "top-ups" or refinancing of small loans, to what can amount to coercion to take out a secured loan to pay off other bills. Selling methods like these can push borrowers into permanent debt. They must be controlled.

It is possible (late-1989) that brokers will be exempted from the Office of Fair Trading licensing regulations. We submitted evidence opposing this in 1988 (7). The change would unfortunately remove one obvious means of control. We urge the lending institutions to regulate such practices. *We recommend that the Office of Fair Trading encourage the use of new contracts governing the commission paid by the lending institution to the broker. The contracts should stipulate that the commission is recoverable if the borrower defaults in the first year, the refund to be set against the borrower's debt.*

At the same time, some lenders do now appreciate the sense of encouraging borrowers who run into financial straits to ask for help and advice. There have been positive efforts by many organisations to improve their contacts with borrowers in difficulties, and then to assess the extent of the problem and offer practical solutions.

High street retailers have often been criticised for their lending and default policies. The National Consumer Council has been among their critics. But while we still have reservations about some of their practices (and we have already looked at in-store promotion of credit accounts in section 5.5.1), there do appear to have been real improvements in their initial debt recovery procedures.

One such initiative is the freephone advice service, such as the one introduced by Burton Financial Services. Some retailers have introduced codes of practice on default procedures: Marks and Spencer's collaboration with the Manchester Money Advice service is a case in point. Others have reviewed and improved staff training in handling arrears and disputes. Some have translated into plain, comprehensible English all their customer information, including arrears and default notices. We applaud all these measures.

There are signs of improvement, too, in the secured lending field. Some creditors now send company staff to visit debtors personally and to make a full assessment of the situation before issuing a summons: Cedar Holdings, for instance, has set up a unit of trained "conciliators".

Ford (13) has been critical of the lack of pre-purchase counselling undertaken by building societies, the fact that they appeared to be somewhat complacent about the build-up of arrears, and were slow to establish a debt recovery procedure. Her study also showed that the lenders seldom had any real knowledge of the circumstances of their defaulters (including their other commitments). This is obviously a worrying state of affairs, particularly in the light of the possible consequences of the rapid rises in mortgage interest rates in 1989/90. We are pleased to see that some building societies are starting to explore with customers in serious arrears the alternatives to repossession: the Abbey National Building society, for instance, has set up a telephone helpline for their customers facing repayment problems.

Few of these models of good practice get the publicity they deserve. When it comes to defaulting customers, lenders no doubt feel some tension between looking firm and intractable and at the same time maintaining good channels of communication. Companies are often coy about revealing the details of their debt collection arrangements.

But it is evident that the creditor organisations that have improved their default systems along the lines we have described do not suffer by it: indeed, more often than not, they are among the market leaders. Most borrowers who are behind with their payments feel guilty, anxious and ashamed: with good systems of communication, trained arrears staff can readily distinguish between the fraudulent and the merely fearful, and can propose solutions. *We urge the credit industry - lenders and their intermediaries - to continue to develop default procedures that encourage customers under financial stress to approach them for help and advice, as the most effective means of debt recovery.*

5.8 Legal action against debtors

The National Consumer Council's major 1989 report on legal services in England and Wales, *Ordinary Justice* (14), included a review of the way courts deal with debt cases. We endorse those recommendations here, and deal only briefly with the same issues.

The Cork Committee on Insolvency said in 1982:

> "There is nothing which can be done in relation to recovery from the debtor who is unemployed and has neither attachable assets nor income."

We agree. In such cases, legal action is expensive and usually fruitless, and the creditor is left further out of pocket. What can be done?

As we have said, appropriate and low-cost credit insurance schemes would be a boon for many who get into difficulties through unemployment or sickness. Better credit risk assessment before lending is another crucial preventive tool. Ensuring that trained, independent money advisers are available to help people sort out their financial disasters is, sometimes literally, a lifesaver. Indeed, we believe that better money advice services are an essential part of the more effective and humane systems of debt enforcement that we propose below.

It is argued that personal bankruptcy should be made easier. Much has been made of the ease with which debtors in the United States can apply for personal bankruptcy, particularly since Federal law was changed in 1978. There are certainly advantages to the debtor in this, not least because the law gives borrowers a fresh start in rebuilding their economic lives once the bankruptcy proceeding is concluded. It has also been suggested that making it easier for consumers to go bankrupt would act as a strong incentive to lenders to check out a borrower's total commitments before deciding to lend them more money.

However, rather than urge reform of bankruptcy procedures at present, we prefer to look to improving the existing methods of debt enforcement.

We have commented on personal multiple debt as an emerging problem. These sorts of debtors cause particular headaches to the courts which are geared to deal mainly with single debts. As we said in *Ordinary Justice*, the only way in which people can have all their debts dealt with together in court is through an "administration order". Here the court sets the total amount of the instalments, and then apportions them pro rata to the different creditors.

Of course, this depends on the court being presented with full details of all the debtor's outstanding commitments, something which seldom happens. Hence the need for more money advisers to guide the debtor and, additionally, to apply for an administration order direct, without the need to obtain a court judgement first. We believe that making sure people are able to get good advice, when they need it, should be a shared responsibility. It would help creditors in cases of multiple debt. It would certainly ease the burden on courts if lay representation were permitted in debt cases. *We therefore urge the Legal Aid Board to take immediate steps to improve the availability of money advice, and central government and the credit industry to supply funding.*

Another bonus of the administration order is that debtors who make regular payments are largely protected from other enforcement actions - the exceptions being disconnection by fuel boards, and repossessions by mortgagees. (We have already commented briefly on these in sections 2.5 and 5.6.) This gives anxious debtors a real breathing space in which to start paying off and a sense of hope that, eventually, the debts will be cleared. *We therefore agree with the Civil Justice Review's proposals that administration orders should be made more widely available and should be shorter in duration.*

Another factor that complicates multiple debt problems is the variety of sanctions available to different creditors.

Sanctions available to different categories of creditor for debt recovery

Type of debt	Sanctions available	In which court
Mortgage arrears	Repossession of home and/or eviction	County court
Rent arrears	Seizure of goods for sale ("distraint"). Repossession of tenant's home and/or eviction	No court* County court
Rate/poll tax arrears	Seizure of goods Imprisonment	Magistrates court
Maintenance arrears	Imprisonment	Magistrates & county court
Fines arrears	Imprisonment	Magistrates
Income tax debt	Imprisonment	County court
Water rates arrears	Disconnection	No court*
Fuel arrears	Disconnection	No court*
Consumer debt	Money judgement. Bailiff's warrant of execution. Seizure of household goods for sale	County court

*No court judgement required; creditor need only apply to the magistrates court for an entry warrant.

As we see, some creditors do not have to act through the court, and have the advantage of being "preferential creditors" - particularly where they can disconnect fuel and power. Other creditors have to go through the courts, even then with no guarantee of repayment. The Touche Ross study found that under a third of debts were paid in full and 28 per cent not at all (15)

This hotchpotch of sanctions for different creditors is inefficient and less than effective. *We recommend that all consumer debts involving less than £25,000 should be dealt with through the county courts.*

References to section 5

1. Committee of Advertising Practice, *The British Code of Advertising Practice*, 8th ed., 1988.
2. Teresa Hinton and Richard Berthoud, *Money Advice Services*, Policy Studies Institute, 1988.

3. Advice Publishing and Training, *Debt Advice in Scotland*: a report prepared for the Scottish Consumer Council, 1988.
4. National Consumer Council, *Money Advice: debt counselling and money advice services training and publications - a summary*, NCC, 1982.
5. National Consumer Council, *A Report on Debt Advice Provision in the UK*, NCC (forthcoming).
6. Office of Fair Trading, *Overindebtedness: a report by the Director General of Fair Trading*, July 1989.
7. National Consumer Council, *Response to the Department of Trade and Industry Review of Consumer Credit Licensing*, NCC, December 1988, PD34/88.
8. *Financial Times*, "Girobank earnings down 8%", 18 July 1989, p.6.
9. Tony Coad, paper given at the conference on Managing International Data Protection in the 1990s, Windsor, October 1989.
10. PAS Business surveys, *Consumers' Use of Credit Survey* for the Office of Fair Trading, 1987.
11. Richard Berthoud and Teresa Hinton, *Credit Unions in the United Kingdom*, Policy Studies Institute, 1989.
12. Nick Huls, "Alternatives to personal bankruptcy", in G. Hormann (ed.) *Verbraucherkredit und Verbraucherinsolvenz*, Bremen, 1986.
13. Janet Ford, *The Indebted Society: credit and default in the 1980s*, Routledge, 1988.
14. National Consumer Council, *Ordinary Justice: legal services and the courts in England and Wales*, HMSO, 1989.
15. Touche Ross Management Consultants, *Study of debt enforcement procedures*, carried out for the Civil Justice Review, Lord Chancellor's Department, December 1986.

Note to the appendices:
Statistics on personal borrowing

We have referred in passing to the difficulty in interpreting aspects of the official financial statistics. There are inaccuracies, for example, in estimating the proportion of retail credit that is included in figures for finance house lending. There are also problems in disaggregating the exact level of secured (non-house purchase) lending taking place within the consumer credit market. The precise statistical problems are not examined in detail again here, but we describe the issues in general terms.

THE SAVINGS RATIO

The problem in calculating the savings ratio is a case in point. At present it is measured as the difference between personal disposable income and consumer spending, and takes no account of any increase in *net assets* (property, pensions, insurance policies, for example). Critics argue that this exaggerates the rise in consumer expenditure, and critically underemphasises income growth.

From a consumer (rather than a macro-economic) point of view, this may create greater concern about credit overcommitment than would actually be justified if net assets were taken into account (although, as we describe below, this is not without its own problems). It is, however, important to keep this in mind when looking at individual and household levels of credit use.

CREDIT CARD LENDING

We referred in the text to the volume of credit card lending as a relatively minor part of the overall market, and also to the increasing numbers who use their cards primarily as a *transaction* instrument. This distinction between those who pay interest charges and "free riders" is important.

Around 45 to 55 per cent of card holders use their cards regularly but incur no interest charges. The published figures on consumer credit outstanding may therefore overestimate the degree of commitment among consumers, since these free riders are included within the monthly statistics. One analyst estimates that if roughly half of credit card lending is within the "transaction only" category, then consumer credit growth will have been *over*estimated by around 2 per cent in 1987, and a similar amount in previous years.

CONSUMER CREDIT AND LENDING FOR HOUSE PURCHASE

By the end of 1988, £267 billion was outstanding to the personal sector, over 84 per cent of which was in mortgages.

We have described some of the tax advantages available to home owners taking on credit commitments. In addition, rising house prices have added to this advantage - one analyst estimates that between 1985 and 1987, this accounted for about 60 per cent of the increase in net wealth. Borrowers have been quick to see the benefit in realising some of this increased value, by taking out further advances against mortgages, or higher mortgages than strictly necessary. This is a sound strategy when prices are rising and interest rates stable. However, between May 1988 and February 1990, average mortgage interest rates rose from 9.5 to 15 per cent. This was accompanied by a fall in house price inflation, especially in the south east of England (*Housing Finance*, no. 4, 1989, p. 6). At the time of writing, there are fears that the depression in the housing market will deepen, and have a greater impact during the early 1990s than had previously been predicted. If this proves correct, the prospects for those people holding large equity mortgages on their homes certainly looks a less prudent decision than they might have expected.

The exact amount of equity leakage from mortgages is unknown. The Finance Houses Association stated in their annual report (1987) that as much as 40 per cent of all new mortgage lending in "recent years" represented equity withdrawal, to finance consumer spending or asset acquisition. Since 1985 around £5.6 billion has been loaned for house purchase, so there is an assumption that £2.2 billion of this was actually "consumer credit". This would add around £10 million to new consumer credit lending in 1988 alone, inflating the figures for outstanding consumer credit.

Other estimates have placed the amount of leakage at anything from £2 billion in 1984 to between £7 billion and £25 billion for 1987.

This "removes" around £55 billion from the £184 billion outstanding on mortgage commitment. However, there is an assumption that most of this is in fact, reinvested. In some cases it is a result of people "trading down" properties as families leave home; lump sums may be reinvested in pension plans, or life assurance policies. The capital may not be entirely "lost" or consumed, but transferred into an illiquid form. Some of the leakage should be considered 'lost', as it is attributed to consumption - new cars, holidays abroad, purchase of expensive consumer durables.

Adjusting the 1987 figures for total outstanding credit, this reduces loans for house purchase to £164 billion (minus around £36 billion for "other" reinvestment) , and increases consumer credit outstanding to £56 billion. This increases the share of consumer credit from about 17 per cent to a quarter of all outstanding personal borrowing - a significant difference.

The figures mentioned here are only estimates, but they illustrate the problems in taking the official figures at face value. They also underline the problems in drawing hard and fast conclusions about the proportionate share of indebtedness between consumers. If credit use is high and expanding amongst those with significant assets - notably property - then theoretically there is less danger of overcommitment. The rising value of the asset is presumed to underwrite the increased credit consumption. However, if "net borrowers" have a different profile from "net investors" or asset-holders, then there is more cause for concern. This was examined in section 3.

Appendix I
Facts and figures

I.1   Real disposable income and real consumers' expenditure, 1982-88

I.2   Outstanding consumer credit, inflation rate and savings ratio

I.3   Personal sector income and expenditure, 1979-88

I.4   Monetary sector: consumer credit, and loans for house purchase, 1979-88

I.5   Changes in credit business of FHA members, 1979-88

I.6   The purposes for which new consumer credit was extended by FHA members, 1984-88

I.7   FHA lending for home improvements and property, 1985-88

I.8   Insurance companies: growth in consumer credit outstanding, 1979-87

I.9   New retail credit extended and retail credit outstanding, 1979-88

I.10 FHA member companies and their retail customers, 1987-88

I.11 DIY spending by volume, 1980-86, two estimates

I.12 Further advances on existing mortgages, 1970-87

I.13 Consumer credit outstanding, by sector, £billion

I.14 Monetary sector: ratio of outstanding lending on consumer credit agreements and lending for house purchase, 1979-87

I.15 Changes in home loans market: debt outstanding, 1979-88

I.16 Sources of mortgage or loan: by socio-economic group of head of household, 1986

I.17 Ten major lenders, by market share, 1988, 1st quarter

I.18 Net lending for house purchase by the monetary sector, 1979-87

I.19 Average prices of houses, and average advances, by lending source, 1981-88

I.20 Credit unions in Northern Ireland and Great Britain, 1986

I.21 Comparison between Northern Ireland and British credit unions

Table I.1 Real disposable income and real consumers' expenditure, 1982-88

Year	Income %	growth per year	Expenditure %
1982	−0.1		0.8
1983	2.2		4.3
1984	2.3		2.2
1985	2.3		3.9
1986	3.4		6.0
1987	2.7		5.2
1988*	3.9		4.0
cumulative 1982-88	16.7		26.4

*Annualised from first quarter figures.

Source: "The UK consumer: savings, debt and the housing market", *The Amex Bank Review*, Special Paper no. 15, September 1988

Table I.2 Outstanding consumer credit, inflation rate and savings ratio

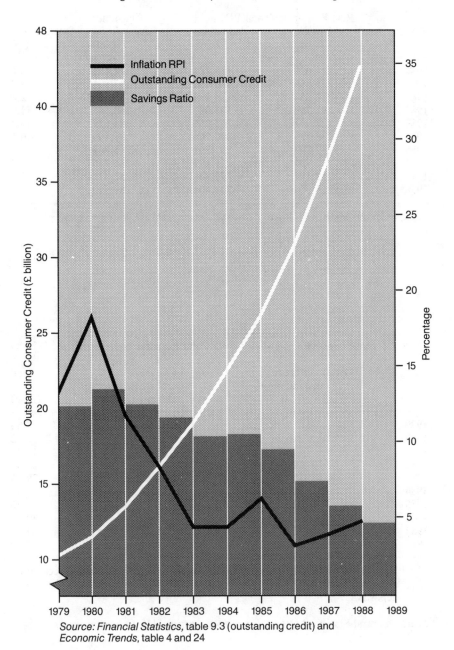

Source: *Financial Statistics*, table 9.3 (outstanding credit) and *Economic Trends*, table 4 and 24

Table I.3 Personal sector income and expenditure, 1979-88

Year	Real PDI at 1985 prices (£m)	Total PDI after deductions (£m)	Consumer expenditure (£m)	Savings ratio (%)
1979	221,673	135,721	118,652	12.6
1980	224,885	160,009	137,896	13.8
1981	222,254	176,084	153,566	12.8
1982	221,709	191,081	168,545	11.8
1983	227,931	205,955	184,619	10.4
1984	232,426	220,764	197,494	10.5
1985	237,802	237,802	215,267	9.5
1986	244,797	255,499	236,756	7.3
1987	252,185	273,306	258,431	5.4
1988*	266,950	303,401	289,840	4.5

Source: Central Statistical Office, *Economic Trends*, HMSO, various years.

Table I.4 Monetary sector: consumer credit, and loans for house purchase, 1979-88

	Consumer credit outstanding [£ bn]	Loans for house purchase [£ bn]	Total [£ bn]
1979	5.48	2.38	7.86
1980	6.74	2.88	9.62
1981	8.79	5.67	14.46
1982	12.60	10.75	23.35
1983	14.80	14.85	29.65
1984	17.42	16.89	34.31
1985	20.35	21.11	41.46
1986	23.97	25.78	49.75
1987	28.81	35.84	64.65
1988	34.39	46.71	81.10

Note: Up to 1981 the *monetary sector* included consumer credit companies recognised as banks. From 1982 it includes consumer credit companies licensed to take deposits.

Source: Central Statistical Office, *Financial Statistics*, HMSO, various years.

Table I.5 Changes in credit business of FHA members, 1979-88

	Credit outstanding at end of period (£ million)			New credit extended during period (£ million)		
	Total	of which consumer credit	(%)	Total	of which consumer credit	(%)
1979	5,989	1,943	(32.4)	4,841	1,698	(35.1)
1980	8,171	2,515	(30.8)	5,224	1,924	(36.8)
1981	10,119	3,008	(29.7)	6,078	2,372	(39.0)
1982	12,144	3,598	(29.6)	7,207	2,909	(40.2)
1983	14,351	4,706	(32.8)	8,101	3,804	(47.0)
1984	17,429	5,881	(33.7)	9,835	4,427	(45.0)
1985	20,622	7,243	(35.1)	11,695	5,034	(43.1)
1986	23,978	9,109	(38.0)	13,386	6,479	(48.4)
1987	28,781	11,569	(40.2)	17,839	9,314	(52.2)
1988	34,111	13,167	(38.6)	23,128	11,283	(48.8)

Source: Finance Houses Association, *Annual Reports* 1983, 1987, 1988 and 1989.

Table I.6 The purposes for which new consumer credit was extended by FHA members, 1984-88

	1984		1985		1986		1987		1988*	
	£m	(%)	£m	(%)	£m	(%)	£m	(%)	£m	(%)
New cars	897	20.3	987	19.6	1,121	17.3	1,540	16.5	1,643	14.6
Used cars	924	20.9	1,011	20.1	1,100	17.0	1,316	14.1	1,650	14.6
Retail credit	499	11.3	609	12.1	622	9.6	706	7.6	} 2,794	24.8
Revolving credit & credit cards	334	7.5	482	9.6	1,044	16.1	1,679	18.0	696	6.2
Home improvements	616	13.9	596	11.8	614	9.5	687	7.4	2,450	21.7
Property	303	6.8	404	8.0	815	12.6	1,941	20.8		
Personal loans	563	12.7	714	14.2	815	12.6	921	9.9	} 2,050*	18.2
Other	291	6.6	231	4.6	348	5.4	524	5.6		
Total	4,427		5,034		6,479		9,314		11,283	

*In 1988 there was a change in the categories used for collecting statistics in the retail credit area. Comparisons are approximate. In addition, 'personal loans' was removed from the categories of lending.

Source: Finance Houses Association, *Annual Reports* 1985, 1987, 1988 and 1989.

Table I.7 FHA lending for home improvements and
property, 1985–88

| | New credit extended | | | |
| | Property | | Home improvements | |
Year	£ million	%	£ million	%
1985	404	(8.0)	596	(11.8)
1986	815	(12.6)	614	(9.5)
1987	1,941	(20.8)	687	(7.4)
1988	2,450	(21.7)	696	(6.2)

(%) = percentage of total new credit extended

Source: Finance Houses Association, *Annual Reports*,
1987, 1988, 1989.

Table I.8 Insurance companies: growth in
consumer credit outstanding,
1979-87

	Credit outstanding (£ million)	Change (%)
1979	240	
1980	271	12.9
1981	299	10.3
1982	317	6.0
1983	356	12.3
1984	*683	92.0
1985	745	9.1
1986	817	9.7
1987	837	2.4
1988	921	10.0

*Introduction of MIRAS in 1983.

Source: Central Statistical Office, *Financial
Statistics*, HMSO, various years.

Table I.9 New retail credit extended and retail credit outstanding, 1979–88

	New credit extended		Outstanding at end of period	
	£ million	% change	£ million	% change
1979	3,020	12.4	1,328	5.5
1980	3,259	7.9	1,630	22.7
1981	3,211	−1.5	1,661	1.9
1982	3,448	7.4	1,757	5.8
1983	3,698	7.3	1,889	7.5
1984	3,864	4.5	2,005	6.1
1985	4,292	11.1	2,200	9.7
1986	4,865	13.4	2,204	0.2
1987	5,286	8.7	2,610	18.4
1988	5,732	8.4	2,895	10.9

Source: Central Statistical Office, *Financial Statistics*, HMSO, various years

Table I.10 FHA member companies and their retail customers, 1987-88

Company	Clients
Marks & Spencer Financial Services Ltd (14% share of retail credit market)	Marks & Spencer
House of Fraser plc (14% share of retail credit market)	Arnotts, Binns, Frasers, Rackhams, Kendals, Cavendish House, Dingles, The Army & Navy, Chanelle, Dickins & Jones, D H Evans, Harrods, Howells, Jollys, David Evans
Trinity House Finance plc	Thorn EMI group, including Rumbelows
Sears Financial Services Ltd (7% share of retail credit market)	Selfridges, Olympus Sports, Adams Childrenswear, Curtess, Freeman Hardy & Willis, Trueform, Dolcis, Saxone, Manfield, Mappin & Webb, Garrard, Fosters Menswear, Wallis Fashions, Lewis's Stores, Millets, Hornes, Lilley & Skinner, and Roland Cartier
Credit & Data Marketing Services Ltd	Littlewoods, also: "Towncards" such as those for Wilmslow, Chester, Tunbridge Wells.
North British Finance Group Ltd	Argos, MFI (and many more)
North West Securities Ltd	C&A, Owen Owen.
Citibank Financial Trust Ltd	Allders, W H Smith "Do-It-All" card
Club 24 Limited (15% share of retail credit market)	Next group, John Kent, Texas HomeCare, Etam, Tandy, Cecil Gee, Great Mills, Lillywhites, Dixons and many smaller schemes
Burton Group Financial Services plc (includes companies owned by Welbeck Finance plc)	Burton group of companies. Debenhams, High & Mighty, Laura Ashley, Russell & Bromley, Portland Holidays, Lunn Poly, Auto Safety Centres.
Lombard North Central plc	Harris Queensway.

Source: Credit Management, July 1987 and September 1988; *Money Observer*, February 1988; and Finance Houses Association, *Annual Reports*, 1987 & 1988.

Table I.11 DIY spending by volume, 1980–86, two estimates

Year	Official estimate (CSO)			Research estimate (VR Ltd)		
	value	volume*	volume index	value	volume*	volume index
1980	1,594	1,594	100	2,424	2,474	100
1981	1,801	1,645	103	2,811	2,615	106
1982	1,926	1,641	103	3,033	2,697	109
1983	2,209	1,782	112	3,456	2,937	119
1984	2,443	1,881	118	3,896	3,179	128
1985	2,756	2,012	127	4,431	3,437	139
1986	3,167	2,207	138	5,037	3,375	151

*1980 prices

Source: Central Statistical Office, *Blue Book*, Tables 4.7 and 4.8, 1987. Verdict Research Ltd, *Verdict on DIY by Retailers*, July 1987.

Table I.12 Further advances on existing mortgages, 1970-87

	Advances on mortgages		As % of total mortgages	
	Number (000s)	Amount (£m)	Number (%)	Amount (%)
1970	79	42	12.7	2.2
1979	293	548	28.2	6.1
1980	273	584	25.3	6.1
1981	325	863	29.5	7.2
1982	443	1,258	33.5	8.4
1983	484	1,466	32.0	7.6
1984	513	1,736	30.9	7.3
1985	511	1,883	30.4	7.1
1986	700	2,814	33.9	7.8
1987	683	2,898	36.2	8.1

Source: Building Societies Association, *Building Society Factbook*, 1988.

Table I.13 Consumer credit outstanding, by sector, £ billion

| | Monetary sector* | credit | | Non-monetary sector credit | Insurance | | |
	Total	card	other	companies	companies	Retailers	Total
1979	5.5	0.9	4.6	2.7	0.2	1.3	9.7
1980	6.7	1.1	5.6	2.8	0.3	1.6	11.6
1981†	10.3	1.6	8.7	1.1	0.3	1.5	13.2
1982	12.6	2.0	10.6	1.3	0.3	1.8	16.0
1983	14.8	2.6	12.2	1.8	0.4	1.9	18.9
1984	17.4	3.3	14.1	2.2	0.7	2.0	22.3
1985	20.4	4.1	16.3	2.8	0.7	2.2	26.1
1986	24.0	5.2	18.8	3.6	0.8	2.2	30.6
1987	28.8	6.0	22.8	4.3	0.8	2.6	36.5
1988	34.4	6.7	27.7	4.6	0.9	2.9	42.8

*Up to 1981 included credit companies recognised as banks.
 From 1982 included credit companies licensed to take deposits.
†Included TSBs.

Source: Central Statistical Office, *Financial Statistics*, HMSO, various years.

Table I.14 Monetary sector: Outstanding lending on consumer credit agreements and lending for house purchase as a percentage of total consumer lending

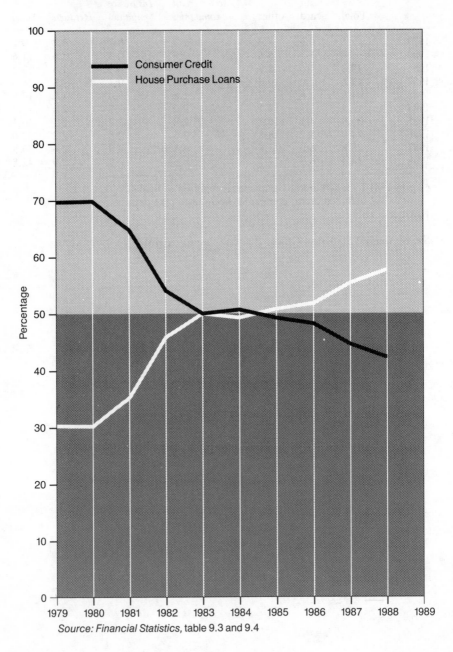

Source: Financial Statistics, table 9.3 and 9.4

Table I.15 Changes in home loans market: debt outstanding, 1979–88

Year	Building societies	Local authorities	Insurance companies (and pension funds) [£ million]	Banks*	TSB	Other public sector	Total
1979	36,986	3,193	1,854	2,380	23	574	45,010
1980	42,708	3,654	2,117	2,870	116	821	52,286
1981	49,039	3,906	2,204	5,640	-	1,169	61,958
1982	57,186	4,468	2,211	10,751	-	1,578	76,194
1983	68,114	4,134	2,336	14,845	-	1,600	91,029
1984	82,686	4,132	2,594	16,888	-	1,716	108,016
					OFIs‡		
1985	97,397	3,632	2,700	21,111	1,136	1,776†	127,752
1986	116,938	3,126	3,135	25,781	3,515	1,837†	154,332
1987	132,328	2,681	3,904	35,836	7,467	1,890†	184,106
1988	157,065	2,382	4,677	45,213	12,475	2,034†	223,846

* Monetary sector   † Central government and public corporations
‡ OFI = other financial institutions

Source: Central Statistical Office, *Financial Statistics*, HMSO, various years.

Table I.16 Source of mortgage or loan: by socio-economic group of head of household, 1986*

Source of mortgage or loan	Professional %	Employers & managers %	Intermediate & junior non-manual %	Skilled manual & own account non-profess. %	Semi-skilled manual & personal service %	Unskilled manual %	All heads of household %
Building society	80	76	84	80	77	82	80
Local authority	2	4	3	9	12	9	6
Insurance company	3	5	4	3	3	2	4
Bank	15	15	9	8	6	5	11
Other source	1	2	1	1	3	2	1
Base for percentages	367	960	809	1,227	336	56	3,755

*Because mortgages or loans can be raised from more than one source, the sum of the percentages may exceed 100 per cent.

Source: General Household Survey, HMSO, 1986.

Table I.17 Ten major mortgage lenders, by market
share, 1989, January-September

	market share %
Halifax Building Society	15.1
Abbey National Building Society	11.4
Nationwide Anglia Building Society	6.0
Leeds Permanent Building Society	5.6
Alliance & Leicester Building Society	4.0
Barclays Bank	3.8
Lloyds Bank	3.6
National Westminster Bank	3.3
Woolwich Equitable Building Society	3.1
National & Provincial Building Society	2.9
Total market share	61.3

Source: Adams Residential Property Index (ARPI), 1989.

Table I.18 Net lending for house purchase by the monetary sector, 1979-87

	1979	1980	1981	1982	1983 [£ millions]	1984	1985	1986	1987
Monetary sector institutions	590	500	2,265	5,078	3,531	2,043	4,223	4,666	10,030
of which CLSB group:	449	375	1,850	4,458	3,708	1,265	2,271	4,102	7,937
Percentage share of new lending market:	9.1%	6.9%	24.3%	35.9%	24.3%	12.0%	22.1%	17.5%	33.9%

Source: Abstract of Banking Statistics, vol.6, May 1989, table 6.31, Statistical Unit, Committee of London and Scottish Bankers.

Table I.19 Average prices of houses, and average advances, by lending source, 1981-88

Year	Building societies		Banks		Insurance companies	
	average price £	advance £	average price £	average advance £	average price £	average advance £
1981	24,200	14,900	. . .	. . .	32,200	18,600
1982	23,600	16,100	. . .	. . .	32,800	19,600
1983	26,500	18,100	35,000	22,500	37,000	22,500
1984	29,100	20,100	45,200	29,000	39,600	23,500
1985	31,100	21,700	47,100	30,900	41,300	25,800
1986	36,300	25,400	48,900	32,900	46,200	30,300
1987	44,220	29,689	49,900	36,600	49,100	34,162
1988	54,279	35,919		39,800	52,200	37,734

Source: Department of the Environment, Scottish Development Department, Welsh Office, *Housing and Construction Statistics*, HMSO, various years.

Table I.20 Credit unions in Northern Ireland and Great Britain, 1986

	N. Ireland (average per union)	Great Britain (average per union)
Membership	1,240	280
Income	£59,560	£7,450
Assets	£532,800	£72,260
Loans to members	£428,620	£62,870

Source: R Berthoud and T Hinton, *Credit Unions in the UK*, Policy Studies Institute, 1989.

Table 1.21 Comparison between Northern Ireland and British credit unions

No. members	Great Britain					Northern Ireland					
	<100	100 – 199	200 – 299	300 – 499	>500	<500	500 – 749	750 – 999	<1000	1000 – 1999	>2000
	(21)	(22)	(11)	(8)	(12)				(64)	(22)	(13)
Loans:											
average advance per member	£120	£150	£170	£290	£310	★	★	★	£250	£290	£340
Loans per member	0.55	0.54	0.45	0.72	0.65	★	★	★	0.48	0.63	0.92
Average per loan	£220	£280	£370	£400	£480	★	★	★	£520	£460	£370
Assets:											
Mean assets per member	£130	£160	£240	£310	£290	£370	£410	£420		£390	£470

★Not available

Source: R. Berthoud and T. Hinton, *Credit Unions in the UK*, Policy Studies Institute, 1989.

Appendix II
Behind the facts

Table II.1 Consumer credit and other personal sector borrowing outstanding, 1980-88

Year	Personal borrowing Lending for house purchase	Consumer credit Monetary sector	(credit cards)	Retailers	Others	Total	Total
	£bn	£ bn		£bn	£bn	£bn	£bn
1980	52.3	6.7	(1.2)	1.6	3.3	11.6	64.0
1981	62.0	10.3	(1.5)	1.7	1.4	13.2	75.2
1982	76.2	12.6	(2.0)	1.8	1.6	16.0	92.2
1983	91.2	14.8	(2.6)	1.9	2.1	18.9	110.1
1984	108.5	17.4	(3.3)	2.0	2.9	22.3	130.8
1985	127.6	20.4	(4.1)	2.2	3.6	26.1	153.7
1986	154.0	24.0	(5.2)	2.2	4.4	30.5	184.6
1987	183.5	28.8	(6.0)	2.6	5.1	36.6	220.1
1988	225.0	34.4	(6.7)	...	...	....	.....

Source: Financial Statistics, nos. 283, November 1985 and 322, February 1989, HMSO.

Table II.2 Credit expenditure on selected items, by age of head of household, UK, 1985

Credit expenditure as a percentage of household spending on:

	clothing and footwear	furniture/ floor coverings	cookers/ washing machines	fridges and freezers	radio/TV and hi-fi	vehicles	holidays	all items*
Age of head of household:	%	%	%	%	%	%	%	%
18-29	14	65	42	63	46	49	24	11
30-39	19	42	81	87	46	51	20	10
40-49	13	43	55	30	38	58	7	9
50-59	10	23	32	40	36	38	16	7
Over 60	7	15	23	15	45	22	13	3
All aged 18 +	13	39	45	52	41	46	16	8

*Includes other items of household expenditure not shown in table.

Source: Social Trends, no. 18, HMSO, 1988.

Table II.3 First-time buyers: income, advance and price, 1979-88

	Advance/price (%)	Price/income	Advance/income
1979	75.7	2.37	1.79
1980	73.8	2.26	1.67
1981	79.1	2.20	1.74
1982	85.1	2.06	1.76
1983	85.1	2.19	1.87
1984	84.7	2.27	1.93
1985	85.3	2.27	1.94
1986	86.1	2.35	2.03
1987	84.7	2.42	2.05
1988	84.8	2.54	2.15

Source: Department of the Environment, Welsh Office, Scottish
Office, *Housing and Construction Statistics* 1976-86, Table 10.11
and Building Societies Association, *Housing Finance*, no. 2
April 1989.

Table II.4 Consumer attitudes to credit, 1987

	Percentage (agreeing strongly)	agreeing strongly/ slightly
You should always try to live within your means	(86)	97
Means you can overspend easily and get into trouble	(86)	97
If you lose your job having credit commitments can make the situation worse	(85)	97
People don't think enough before taking out credit	(62)	90
Obtaining credit cards is far too easy these days	(70)	91
The amount of credit you get should be linked to the amount you earn	(74)	92
Credit limits should be increased only at the customer's request	(64)	84
Having credit saves you carrying a lot of cash	(46)	82
There should be tighter controls on credit advertising	(57)	79
A deposit should be required before taking out credit	(43)	69
Credit increases people's expectations	(37)	79

Source: Office of Fair Trading, *Consumers' Use of Credit Survey*, PAS Business
Surveys, 1987.

Table II.5 Reasons for using credit, by age, social class and presence of young children in household, 1987

	Age						Social class				Children		
	18-24	25-34	35-44	45-54	55-64	65+	AB	C1	C2	DE	children under 16	no children under 16	Total
Base	128	369	338	228	186	100	249	306	364	368	577	772	1349
	%	%	%	%	%	%	%	%	%	%	%	%	%
Convenience	32	49	47	55	69	76	61	56	50	43	45	57	52
Necessity	58	41	35	35	20	10	26	31	37	49	43	31	36
Economy	13	18	22	17	13	16	28	19	17	7	18	17	17
Flexibility	16	19	16	15	12	11	15	14	16	18	19	14	16
Other	2	4	3	2	3	2	3	3	4	1	3	3	3

Source: Office of Fair Trading, *Consumers' Use of Credit Survey*, PAS Business Surveys, 1987.

Table II.6 Reasons for using credit, by personal income and employment status, 1987

| | Total | Income per annum | | | | | | | Employment status | | | | | | |
		Nil	up to £2,500	£2,501-£5,000	£5,001-£10,000	£10,001-£15,000	£15,001-20,000	over £20,000	self-employed/full-time	part-time	full-time student	unemployed under 6 months	unemployed over 6 months	retired	f/t housework
Base	1,349	85	352	224	288	144	75	53	632	220	12	17	50	115	267
	%	%	%	%	%	%	%	%	%	%	%	%	%	%	%
Convenience	52	64	50	44	47	61	62	44	50	49	18	42	34	78	55
Necessity	36	30	39	45	43	29	21	21	37	37	73	52	64	10	36
Economy	17	20	13	12	17	18	26	38	20	14	23	10	6	14	15
Flexibility	16	16	15	17	18	15	17	6	16	21	-	10	18	10	14
Other	3	1	4	2	2	4	2	9	3	5	-	-	4	1	3

Source: Office of Fair Trading, *Consumers' Use of Credit Survey*, PAS Business Surveys, 1987.

Table II.7 Electricity disconnections for non-
           payment, England and Wales
           (domestic credit customers)

	Number	Level of disconnections [1979-80 = 100]
1979-80	98,894	100
1980-81	118,221	119
1981-82	108,266	109
1982-83	91,334	92
1983-84	90,722	92
1984-85	91,039	92
1985-86	102,714	104
1986-87	98,823	100
1987-88	88,910	90
1988-89	75,230	76

Source: Electricity Consumers' Council.

Table II.8 Gas disconnections for non-payment,
           England, Scotland and Wales

	Number	Level of disconnection [1979 = 100]
1979	35,166	100
1980	41,846	119
1981	28,725	88
1982	28,813	88
1983	30,971	94
1984	33,768	103
1985	35,626	109
1986	45,255	136
1987	60,778	170
1988	48,037	149

Source: Gas Consumers Council.

Table II.9 Household disconnections for non-
payment of water rates by non-
statutory companies, England

	Number	Level of disconnection [1984-85 = 100]
1984-85	2,052	100
1985-86	4,212	205
1986-87	6,450	314
1987-88	7,120	347
1988-89	...	...

Source: Hansard 19 July 1988, col. 527.

Table II.10 Local authority rent arrears, England and
Wales, 1977-86

	Former tenant (£m)	Present tenant (£m)	% Total collectable rent
1977	44.5	-	3.0
1978	62.0	-	3.1
1979	61.1	-	3.5
1980	73.8	-	3.8
1981	100.0	-	4.4
1982	28.4	102.5	4.3
1983	39.6	127.3	4.9
1984	43.0	134.1	5.1
1985	49.0	149.0	5.4
1986	54.5	151.1	5.8

Source: Chartered Institute of Public Finance and
Accountancy, *CIPFA Housing Revenue Accounts
Statistics.*

Table II.11 The nature and size of plaints in the county court, 1987

Nature of plaint	% of all	size of debt				
		<£100	£101-£500	£501-1,000	£1,000-£2,000	>£2,000
(Base=2,375,431 plaints)						
Goods sold and delivered, work done, materials supplied, professional fees etc.	64.0	33.7	42.6	11.3	8.0	4.1
Moneylenders' claims (excluding mortgages)	1.6	13.0	36.3	20.1	20.0	10.0
Bank loans (bank or finance house)	11.2	6.3	31.1	19.9	25.0	17.4
Recovery of land	7.0	2.5	12.2	7.5	7.0	4.8
Miscellaneous	2.7					
Other claims for debt, e.g. income tax, dishonoured cheques, arrears of rent (excl. HP)	6.5	17.8	34.6	18.5	17.5	10.9
All plaints	100	24.9	37.4	12.7	11.1	7.3

Source: Judicial Statistics Annual Report, 1987.

Table II.12 Attachment of earnings, applications and orders
1980-87

	Application filed	Orders made	Orders made/ applications filed (%)
1979	85,612	42,971	50.2
1980	80,527	38,677	48.0
1981	70,359	32,197	45.8
1982	71,708	35,087	48.9
1983	79,280	42,612	53.8
1984	97,113	57,619	59.3
1985	106,361	64,756	60.9
1986	103,407	58,912	57.0
1987	103,382	53,297	51.6

Source: Judicial Statistics, 1979-1987.

Appendix III
Consumer concerns

III.1   The percentage changes in building society repossessions, and house prices, 1970-88

III.2   Building society arrears, 1979-88

III.3   Credit (excluding mortgage) repayments, by households with different housing tenures 1986

III.4   Weekly credit and mortgage commitments of those buying their homes, by income, 1986

III.5   Local authority and building society mortgage repossessions and arrears, England, 1980-88

III.6   Households accepted for rehousing by local authorities where main reason is mortgage default or arrears, England and Wales, 1979-88

III.7   Personal sector debt: income and debt: wealth ratios, 1971-1987/88

III.8   Investment income, by type of investment and household income, 1986

III.9   Age distribution of mortgage-holding investors and borrowers, 1989

III.10   Relationship between credit commitment and income, 1987

III.11   Relationship between personal/joint credit commitments and selected assets, 1987

III.12   Profile of those thinking their current commitments are too high

III.13   Profile of those taking on commitments they had later regretted

III.14   Profile of those having difficulty in keeping up credit repayments in past five years

III.15   Types of credit that respondents had had difficulty repaying by length of unemployment

III.16   The percentage of households in twelve income groups making credit repayments of £25 a week or more, 1982-86

III.17   Elderly people's use of credit

III.18   Perceived advantages and disadvantages of credit cards

III.1   The percentage changes in building society repossessions, and house prices,
1970-88

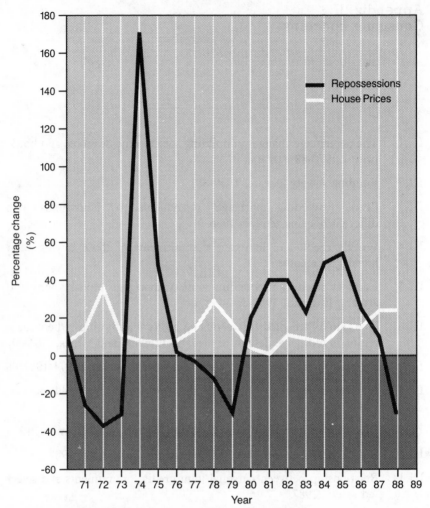

Source: Repossessions: Building Societies Association, *Mortgage
Repayment Difficulties,* 1985 and Council of Mortgage Lenders, *Housing
Finance,* no. 3 July 1989, House prices: *Housing Finance,* no. 3 July 1989

Table III.2 Building society arrears, 1979-89

Year	Number of loans at end of period	Loans 6-12 months in arrears end of period		Loans over 12 months in arrears end of period	
		Number	(%)	Number	(%)
1979	5,264,000	8,420	0.16		
1980	5,396,000	13,490	0.25		
1981	5,505,000	18,720	0.34		
1982	5,664,000	23,790	0.42	4,810	0.085
1983	5,949,000	25,580	0.43	6,540	0.11
1984	6,354,000	41,940	0.66	8,260	0.13
1985	6,705,000	49,620	0.74	11,400	0.17
1986	7,071,000	45,250	0.64	11,310	0.16
1987	7,197,000	48,220	0.67	13,000	0.18
1988	7,441,010	37,200	0.50	8,930	0.12
1989	7,955,000	58,380	0.73	12,100	0.15

Source: Building Societies Association, *Housing Finance*, April 1989. Council of Mortgage Lenders, February 1990.

Table III.3 Credit (excluding mortgage) repayments, by households with different housing tenures, 1986

	No. with repayments (%)	Mean repayment (£ pw)
All	37.9	£18.3
Rented	27.0	£12.4
Owned on mortgage	57.5	£21.0
Owned outright	16.8	£16.9
Other	31.9	*

*Numbers too small to be reliable

Source: OFT/FES (1986)

Table III.4 Weekly credit and mortgage
commitments of those buy-
ing their homes, by income,
1986

	Mean weekly instalments
All households	£31.70
Weekly income	
£80- 99	£23.30
£100-124	£21.00
£125-149	£20.70
£150-174	£23.20
£175-199	£24.40
£200-224	£24.00
£225-249	£27.20
£250-299	£27.30
£300-349	£31.20
£350-399	£31.70
£400-499	£38.70
£500-plus	£48.40

Source: OFT/FES (1986)

Table III.5 Local authority and building society mortgage repossessions and arrears, England, 1980-88

	Number	% of loans	*[Building societies]
1980-81	1,000	0.14	0.056
1981-82	1,100	0.16	0.077
1982-83	950	0.14	0.105
1983-84	840	0.13	0.123
1984-85	570	0.10	0.171
1985-86	630	0.13	0.250
1986-87	490	0.12	0.296
1987-88	330	0.10	0.319
1988-89			0.216

*Building society figures for comparison.

Source: Hansard 6 March 1989, col.428.

Table III.6 Households accepted for rehousing by local
authorities where main reason is mortgage
default or arrears, England and Wales, 1979-88

Year	Households	% of acceptances
1979	2,000	4
1980	2,500	4
1981	3,600	5
1982	4,400	6
1983	4,800	6
1984	6,300	8
1985	8,600	9
1986	10,200	10
1987	10,600	9
June 87-88	9,800	

Source: Hansard 27 June 1988, col.146; 25 October 1988,
col.144.

III.7   Personal sector debt:income and debt:wealth ratios, 1971-1987/88

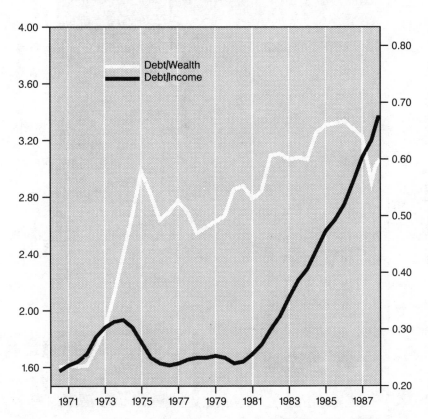

Source: London Business School, *Economic Outlook 1987-91*, July 1988.

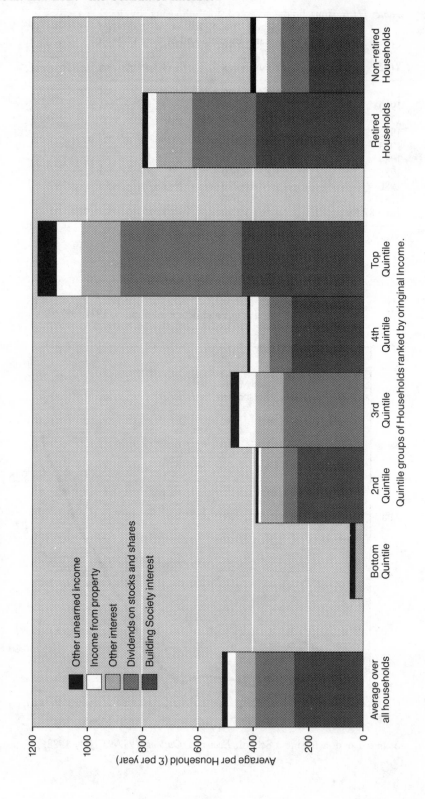

III.8   Investment income, by type of investment and household income, 1986

Table III.9 Age distribution of mortgage holding investors and borrowers, 1989

Age	Investors By number (%)	By amount (%)	Borrowers (%)
16-19	6	0.6	0.5
20-24	10	4	7
25-34	22	13	31
35-54	33	27	50
55-64	13	23	8
65+	16	33	3

Source: Building Societies Association, personal
communication. (figures adjusted to the
nearest '000)

Table III.10 Relationship between credit commitment and income, 1987

	£1-5,000	personal gross annual income including partner's if applicable £5,001- £10,000	£10,001- £15,000	£15,001- £20,000	over £20,000
Base: all respondents (weighted)	(633)	(555)	(283)	(187)	(243)
Amount owed on credit excluding 1st mortgage	%	%	%	%	%
Use credit but owe nil	11	13	14	17	19
Use credit, and owe	28	52	54	59	67
Up to £200	15	24	15	16	9
£201-£500	6	11	12	14	13
£501-£1,000	2	6	7	10	10
£1,001-£2,000	2	6	7	6	10
£2,001-£5,000	*	4	8	10	13
£5,000 plus	*	*	4	3	10
Mean amount (£)	£280-£400	£590	£1,130	£990	£1,850
Do not use credit	59	32	27	17	13
Refused/DK/NS	2	3	6	8	3

*=less than 1%

Source: OFT/PAS 1987.

Table III.11 Relationship between personal/joint credit commitments and selected assets, 1987

Assets held	Total	Personal and/or joint commitments					
		Nil	£500	£501-£1,000	£1,001-£2,000	£2,001-£5,000	£5,000
	%	%	%	%	%	%	%
Stocks, shares unit trusts	21	42	21	20	25	27	42
Building society savings a/c	58	71	56	63	64	75	73
Savings certificates	7	10	4	5	2	4	11
Bank current account	70	86	69	88	94	92	89
Premium bonds	32	43	29	32	34	44	44
Life assurance	54	58	60	70	75	81	80
PO account	14	16	12	19	16	11	23
Property other than home (includes timeshare)	4	7	3	5	6	7	13

Source: OFT/PAS, 1988

Table III.12 Profile of those thinking their current commitments are too
high (number = 185, 9 per cent of total sample)

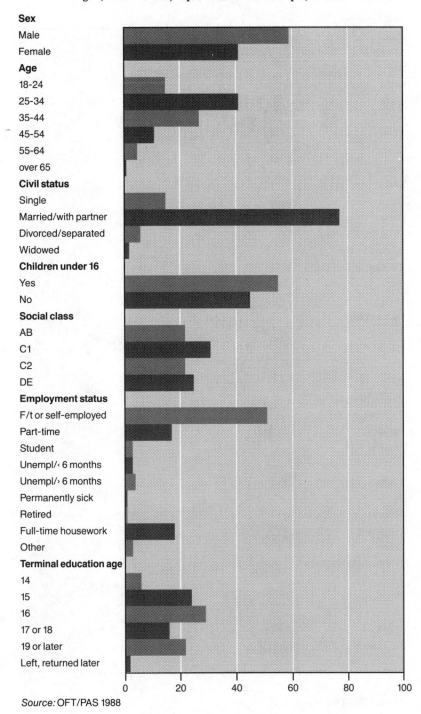

Sex
Male
Female
Age
18-24
25-34
35-44
45-54
55-64
over 65
Civil status
Single
Married/with partner
Divorced/separated
Widowed
Children under 16
Yes
No
Social class
AB
C1
C2
DE
Employment status
F/t or self-employed
Part-time
Student
Unempl/< 6 months
Unempl/> 6 months
Permanently sick
Retired
Full-time housework
Other
Terminal education age
14
15
16
17 or 18
19 or later
Left, returned later

0   20   40   60   80   100

Source: OFT/PAS 1988

Table III.13 Profile of those taking on commitments they had later regretted
(number = 418, 19 per cent of total sample)

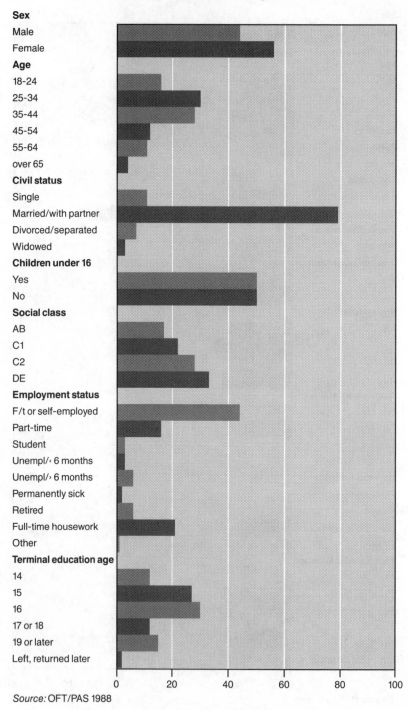

Source: OFT/PAS 1988

Table III.14 Profile of those having difficulty in keeping up credit repayments
in past five years (number = 227)

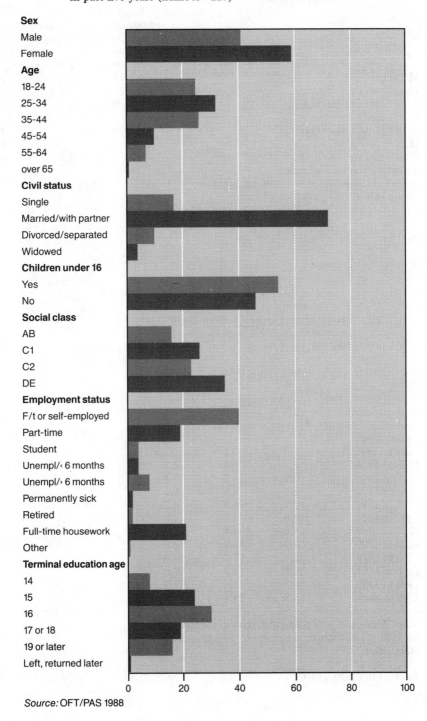

Source: OFT/PAS 1988

Table III.15 Types of credit that respondents had had difficulty repaying, by length of unemployment

	Unemployed <6 months (%)	Unemployed >6 months (%)
Mortgage	13	5
Loan from bank/b.s.	24	23
Loan from finance company	9	26
Credit cards	-	35
Credit/budget store cards	28	4
H.P.	6	13
Check trading	-	9
Tallyman/doorstep salesmen	-	7

Source: OFT/PAS, 1987 (small sample).

Table III.16 The percentage of households in twelve income groups making credit repayments of £25 a week or more, 1982–86

	1982 %	1984 %	1986 %
All households	3.3	5.9	9.4
Income group:			
£80 to £99	0.4	0.2	-
£100 to £124	0.8	1.6	2.1
£125 to £149	0.7	1.2	3.3
£150 to £174	2.6	3.6	6.1
£175 to £199	2.9	4.8	4.2
£200 to £224	2.0	7.1	4.8
£225 to £249	5.0	5.4	9.9
£250 to £299	7.9	7.8	11.8
£300 to £349	8.1	13.0	16.0
£350 to £399	10.5	18.2	19.6
£400 to £499	18.3	21.4	27.3
£500 or more	13.3	23.1	27.9

Note: Because of processing differences, the figures for 1982 are not strictly comparable with those for other years.

Source: OFT/FES (1986).

Table III.17 Elderly people's use of credit

	[Total]	Used in last 5 years (%)	Used nowadays (%)	[Total]
Mortgage	38	5	3	34
Bank/b.s. loan	24	4	1	12
Credit cards	37	20	17	32
Credit store card	14	4	3	10
Mail order	30	9	7	23
None of these	23	63	72	31

Source: OFT/PAS, 1987.

Table III.18 Perceived advantages and disadvantages of credit cards

	Access & Visa (%)	Store & budget cards (%)
Don't have to have personal contact with the creditor	33	10
Can pay as much or as little as you wish	33	8
Minimum monthly payment	41	10
Pay all off if you wish	42	17
Easy to obtain	38	18
Convenient to use	50	17
Can usually increase credit limit on request	35	10
You know what payments are going to be, so you can budget for it	20	11
You have to make a minimum payment each month	24	11
Because of the amount of interest you have to pay	21	15
Because it encourages impulse buying	68	39

Source: OFT/PAS 1988.

Appendix IV
Credit referencing

Appendix IV.1
Credit Account Information Sharing (CAIS): voluntary code of practice

ABOUT CCN

CCN Systems Ltd. was formed in 1980 and is a wholly owned subsidiary of one of Britain's leading commercial organisations. CCN supply credit information and credit related services to commercial organisations all over the world. CCN employ over 800 people and its annual turnover is approximately £30 million. It has offices in Nottingham, Manchester, London, Amsterdam and Atlanta, Georgia (USA).

CCN has been granted a licence by the Office of Fair Trading to carry on business as a Credit Reference Agency, and it is the leading provider of consumer credit information in the United Kingdom.

THE PURPOSE OF CAIS

The purpose of CAIS is to provide credit companies with an independent and accurate source of information on the existing and past credit commitments of people who have applied to them for the provision of credit or other financial services.

HOW THE CAIS SCHEME OPERATES

Participating companies send information on all their credit customers each month to CCN which pools the data onto a computer file. Participating companies search the file for information on the credit history and credit commitments of persons who have applied to them for credit or other financial services. This information enables companies to more accurately assess the creditworthiness of their credit applicants.

WHY THE CAIS SCHEME WAS ESTABLISHED

Consumer credit granting companies advance credit to individuals to finance the purchase of goods or services. A primary concern of these companies is to ensure that they grant credit to applicants who will repay and avoid giving credit to applicants who will not repay. The accurate assessment of credit applications can be a difficult task and credit companies do not make the right decision in every case. Incorrect credit decisions can be broken down into two categories: giving credit to applicants who do not repay, and refusing credit to applicants who would have repaid.

No company and no credit system can avoid making mistakes of this kind, but it is clearly in the interests of both lender and borrower that the number of such mistakes is minimised. To achieve this, credit companies must have access to accurate information, and efficient systems for processing and evaluating that information, at the time they make credit decisions.

The last five years have seen major changes in the information used by credit companies and the systems they employ to assess credit applications:

Information

Traditionally credit companies have based their lending decisions on the information supplied by prospective customers on application forms, combined with additional information obtained from a Credit Reference Agency. Although this information is highly valuable, it has not enabled lenders to prevent a sharp increase in the proportion of defaulting accounts which many of them have experienced over recent years.

The CAIS scheme was established in order to provide lenders with a central source of additional information to enable them to make better and more informed lending decisions and to reduce the number of incorrect decisions they make.

Systems

The most significant development in credit assessment methods to take place over the past five years has been the movement away from subjective or judgmental systems towards a more objective approach using credit scoring systems. It is not the purpose of this document, nor is it CCN's intention, to lay down rules governing the way in which participating companies incorporate CAIS information into their decision making procedures. It is CCN's view, however, that credit scoring techniques represent the fairest and most accurate credit assessment method available, and that they are ideally suited to the task of evaluating the quantity and detailed nature of the data made available by the CAIS scheme.

THE BENEFITS OF CAIS TO THE CONSUMER

The CAIS scheme provides important benefits to the consumer:

1) Credit becomes more available to people who will repay and less available to others.
2) By providing access to a person's credit track-record, credit decisions can be made faster and with less red tape.
3) Consumers can be prevented from taking on financial commitments which they can not afford.
4) The great majority of information contained in the CAIS file relates to accounts which have a satisfactory payment record. In many cases the availability of this information leads to the acceptance of applications which might otherwise have been turned down.
5) CAIS can keep down lenders' costs by providing them with the means of lowering their numbers of defaulting accounts. In this way, CAIS can reduce the costs to consumers of obtaining credit.

COMPANIES ELIGIBLE FOR MEMBERSHIP OF THE SCHEME

To qualify for membership of the CAIS scheme companies must satisfy the following requirements:
1) They must hold a licence issued by the Office of Fair Trading allowing them to provide consumer credit services.
2) During the period in which they are members of the CAIS scheme they must comply fully with the regulations governing the behaviour of members set out in this document.
3) They must make their credit files freely available under the scheme to all participating companies.
4) They must sign a written agreement accepting the terms and conditions governing their participation in the scheme.
5) The membership of a participating company will be terminated and its data removed from the CAIS file if in the reasonable opinion of CCN:
    (i) That company no longer satisfies the rules for membership of the scheme as set out in this document.
    (ii) It is no longer in the public interest for that company to continue to be a member of the scheme.
    (iii) The company has committed a serious breach of the rules of the scheme and has failed to rectify the situation within 28 days after being asked to do so in writing by CCN.

INFORMATION PROVIDED TO PARTICIPATING COMPANIES

1) The data provided to participating companies under the scheme is factual. No opinions are expressed on the information.
2) When CAIS information is presented to users, the name of the participating company which provided the information is not disclosed. Only a general description of the type of company to which the information relates is provided - for example, Retailer, Bank, Finance House, Credit Card Company, Mail Order Company.

3) All information held on the CAIS file relates to a named individual. To obtain information about an individual, participating companies must make a specific request for information relating to that person.

4) The information supplied to participating companies is intended to help them make an accurate assessment of a person's creditworthiness and can be summarised as follows:
   (i) The name and address of the individual in whose name an account is filed.
   (ii) The type of company to which an account relates.
   (iii) The type of account (e.g. credit card, hire purchase).
   (iv) Financial details of the account (e.g. balance outstanding, repayment terms, credit limit).
   (v) A summary of the payment history on the account.
   (vi) The date when the account was last updated on the CAIS file.
   (vii) The individual's total current credit commitments recorded on the CAIS file.

THE INTEGRITY OF CAIS INFORMATION

The success of the CAIS scheme depends on it having the confidence of the public and the credit industry. To merit this confidence, it must be evident that tight controls are exercised to protect the integrity of the CAIS information. This places a duty on the participating companies and CCN.

Obligations of Participating Companies

Under the rules of the CAIS scheme participating companies are required to:

1) Take every reasonable precaution to ensure that the information supplied to CCN for use in the scheme is accurate and up-to-date.

2) Inform CCN of any inaccuracies in the data provided by them, and take the necessary steps to ensure that the mistake is corrected in the files subsequently provided to CCN.

3) Provide CCN every month with information enabling CCN to update the CAIS file.

4) Use the CAIS information for the sole purpose of helping to assess the creditworthiness of persons who have applied to them for the provision of credit or other financial services.

5) Not disclose CAIS information belonging to another participating company to any person who does not have a genuine and legitimate right of access to the information.

6) Comply with the standard procedures for describing and classifying information in use throughout the scheme, which are laid down by CCN and used by all other participating companies.

7) Take all reasonable measures to ensure that its employees and agents strictly comply with the rules of the scheme.

Obligations of CCN

CCN is required to:

1) Use the information provided by participating companies for the sole purpose of operating the CAIS scheme (as outlined in this document) and for no other purpose whatsoever.

2) Provide efficient computerised systems for the collection, storage and updating of the credit information supplied by participating companies, and ensure that this information is safeguarded by stringent security controls.

3) Provide efficient computer systems which enable information from the CAIS file to be accessed by participating companies in a fast, convenient and accurate manner.

4) Supply CAIS information to participating companies in a form and manner which can be easily understood.

5) Correct any inaccuracies within 28 days after receiving satisfactory written evidence that inaccurate information is stored on the CAIS file. CCN will also send to a consumer written confirmation that a correction has been made to the CAIS file within 7 days after the information has been corrected.

6) Restrict access to CAIS information to authorised users only.

7) Take all reasonable measures to ensure that its employees and agents strictly comply with the rules of the scheme.

CAIS AND THE LAW

The law lays down strict regulations governing the activities of Credit Reference Agencies. These regulations are embodied in the Consumer Credit Act 1974 and the Data Protection Act 1984. The rules of the CAIS scheme require that both CCN and the participating companies comply strictly with the spirit and the letter of the regulations affecting the operation of the scheme. A layman's guide to these regulations is set out below:

Registration

CCN has filed with the Data Protection Registrar a general statement outlining:
- the purpose of the CAIS file,
- the contents of the file,
- and the source of the CAIS information.

This information is to be made available in Public Libraries for inspection by the public.

Disclosure

(i) A private individual is entitled to apply to CCN in writing, and enclosing the appropriate fee, for a copy of the information which CCN holds in its files for that person.

(ii) CCN must provide to that individual, within seven working days, a detailed explanation of all the information which it holds in its files at the individual's address.

(iii) The information provided to individuals by CCN must be accompanied by an explanation of the actions a consumer can take if he feels that the information filed by CCN is inaccurate.

(iv) If a consumer claims that inaccurate information is recorded in CCN's files, CCN must either:
- delete or amend the information,
- or file a "notice of correction" supplied by the consumer, and provide the notice to companies who request information on that person.

(v) If a consumer is not satisfied that inaccurate information on CCN's file has been remedied, there is a statutory right of recourse to the Office of Fair Trading.

General Rules

A number of additional rules of a more general nature are laid down:

(i) CAIS information must be obtained fairly and lawfully.

(ii) CAIS information must be used for the purpose of operating the CAIS system and for no other purpose.

(iii) CAIS information should be adequate, relevant and not excessive in relation to the purpose it was obtained.

(iv) CAIS data should be accurate and kept up-to-date.

(v) CAIS data must not be kept for longer than necessary.

(vi) Appropriate security measures must be taken against unauthorised access to, or alteration, disclosure or destruction of, CAIS information and against accidental loss or destruction of CAIS information.

Appendix IV.2
Examples of the information on a full credit reference

The names, addresses and credit reference information on the following file are fictitious. We are grateful to CCN Systems for preparing the example for us.

CCN Systems

CCN Reference No. – quote on all correspondence:

CCN Systems Limited   **Consumer and Legal Affairs Department**

──────────────── CONSUMER CREDIT ACT 1974 ────────────────

Please complete **Part A** of this form. You are entitled to see all information **(up to six years)**. If this Agency keeps information relating to you it will be entered in **Part B** and returned to you.

Date

A

I wish to apply under Section 158(1) of the above Act for a copy of the file (if any) you keep relating to me. **I enclose a postal order/cheque for £1** to cover the statutory fee **(do not send stamps or cash)**.

Signed ....

1ST PREVIOUS ADDRESS (if lived at in last 6 yrs.)

MONTH   YEAR   MONTH   YEAR

FROM _____ TO _____

ADDRESS _____

_____

POSTAL TOWN _____

COUNTY _____ P.O. CODE _____

PRESENT NAME & ADDRESS

SURNAME ____ ANYBODY ____ MR/MRS/MISS

FORENAMES ___ JOHN ___

ADDRESS ___ 37 SHINBROOK AVENUE ___

___ DALTON ___

POSTAL TOWN ___ HUDDERSFIELD ___

COUNTY _WEST YORKSHIRE_ P.O. CODE ___

2ND PREVIOUS ADDRESS (if lived at in last 6 yrs.)

MONTH   YEAR   MONTH   YEAR

FROM _____ TO _____

ADDRESS _____

_____

POSTAL TOWN _____

COUNTY _____ P.O. CODE _____

PLEASE READ STATEMENT OF CONSUMER'S RIGHTS OVERLEAF

B

(For office use only)

Present Address

Confirmed on the electoral roll since 1986

John ANYBODY

Judgment

Mr John Anybody
Date 12/86, Amount £391, Case Number 8472124,
Court - Leeds, Source LCH

Registration: London 653331

178 R8/89

SCHEDULE 1   (Regulation 2)

CREDIT REFERENCE AGENCY FILES

CONSUMER'S RIGHTS UNDER SECTION 159 OF THE

CONSUMER CREDIT ACT 1974

1. With this statement is a copy of the credit reference agency's file on you.

Your rights if an entry is wrong

2. If you think that anything in the file is wrong and you are likely to suffer as a result, you have the following rights.

3. If you think that there is no basis at all for the entry, you may write to the agency requiring it to remove the entry.

4. If the entry is incorrect you may write to the agency requiring it to remove or amend the entry. When writing to the agency, you should say why you think that the entry is incorrect.

What happens then?

5. Within 28 days of receiving your letter the agency should write and tell you that it has removed the entry from the file, or amended it, or taken no action. If the entry has been amended, the agency must send you a copy of the amended entry.

What can you do if you are not satisfied?

6. If the agency tells you that it has taken no action, or if it does not reply to your letter within the 28 days, or if it makes an amendment which you think is unsatisfactory, you may write a note correcting the entry and send it to the agency with a letter requiring the agency —

to add the note to its file about you

and

to include a copy of it when furnishing information included in or based on the entry which it corrects.

7. Your note of correction should give a clear and accurate explanation of why you consider the entry to be incorrect. It must not be more than 200 words long. You can prepare the note yourself or with the help of, for example, a citizens' advice bureau, a consumer advice centre or a solicitor.

N.B. If the agency considers that your note of correction is incorrect or defamatory, or frivolous, or scandalous, or unsuitable for any other reason, it can ask the Director General of Fair Trading to give a ruling as to what it must do.

IMPORTANT

8. If the agency has replied to the first letter in which you object to the entry, you must send your note of correction within 28 days of receiving its reply.

9. If the agency did not reply to your first letter within 28 days, your note of correction must be sent within the next 28 days.

10. If the agency accepts your note of correction (i.e. is not seeking a ruling from the Director General), it must tell you within 28 days that it intends to comply with your request.

Your rights if the agency does not accept your note of correction within 28 days

11. You may write to the Director General of Fair Trading at the Office of Fair Trading, Field House, Bream's Buildings, London EC4A 1PR, who may make whatever order he thinks fit. You should say that you are writing under Section 159(5) of the Consumer Credit Act 1974 and give:

your full name and address (and telephone number, if any);

name and address of the credit reference agency;

the agency's reference number (if any);

details of the entry you consider incorrect, including:

why you consider it incorrect;

why you consider if prejudicial to your interests, and an indication of when you sent to the agency the note of correction mentioned in paragraph 6.

Before deciding what to do, the Director General may ask the agency for its side of the case by sending it a copy of your letter. In return, you will be sent any comments the agency makes.

NOTE: The various periods of 28 days referred to in this statement start with the day following receipt and end with that of delivery, so in order to avoid any risk of losing your rights you should allow for postal delays.

- 2 -

IMPORTANT NOTE

CCN Systems Ltd stores and supplies information about individuals according to address. Because of this, information about other persons living, or who have lived at your address, could be supplied to a credit grantor making an enquiry about you. It should be clear to credit grantors using the file what information refers to you as the subject of the enquiry. The Office of Fair Trading has advised us that the Consumer Credit Act 1974 requires us to provide you with all the information which a credit grantor could obtain from us on enquiry about you or your address, whether that information relates to you or to other persons who live, or have lived, at your address.

Present Address

Confirmed on the electoral roll since 1986

      Mary ANYBODY

Judgment

Mr A.N. OTHER
Date 05/85, Amount £217, Case Number 8212620,
Court - Sheffield, Source LCH

– 3 –

CREDIT ACCOUNT INFORMATION SHARING ("CAIS")

CCN Systems Limited operates, on behalf of its clients, a credit account information sharing scheme — "CAIS". This service is only open to lenders who contribute details of their customer's good and bad credit histories. It has the advantage of making it easier, quicker and cheaper for the consumer who has a good credit history to obtain credit facilities. Such a scheme is a contribution to the call by the Office of Fair Trading and consumer organisations for responsible lending as it helps prevent overcommitment. The information shown on the following pages is taken from the lenders' computerised accounts file and where appropriate is brought up to date each month when they send a computer tape to CCN Systems Limited. **ANY QUERY ABOUT THIS INFORMATION SHOULD BE MADE FIRST TO THE COMPANY SHOWN AS PROVIDING THE INFORMATION — CCN SYSTEMS LIMITED CANNOT CHANGE THE INFORMATION HELD ON ITS CLIENT'S COMPUTERS.**

When reading the information that follows, the account status codes shown have the following meanings:—

Account status code	Meaning
1	Satisfactory Paying Account
2	Payment approximately 1–2 months late
3	Payment 3 or more months late
4	Account status not known
8	Defaulted account
9	Written off account

The status history shows a list of account status codes for the past year, with the most recent previous month on the left and the oldest previous month on the right. For example:—

Current status   1
Status history   2.2.1.1.1.1.1.1.4.4

The current status of '1' shows that when the account details were last updated the account was satisfactory paying. The status history shows that the month before that the account was paid from 1–2 months late, but 3 months before the account was satisfactory paying. Nine months ago the account status was not known.

CAIS Account Details

Present Address

Mr J Anybody, Dudbuy,   Rental, Monthly payment £20, Opened 06/86,
Balance Nil.

Current Status   1
Status History   1.1.1.1.1.1.1.1.1.1.1.1.
Total Status 2 in last 14 months   =   0
Total Status 3 in last 14 months   =   0
The above information was last updated on   03.12.89

Mrs M Anybody, Wouldbe Bros., Defaulted Account,
Amount of Debt at 10/89, £30

Current Status   9
Status History
Total Status 2 in last   months   =
Total Status 3 in last   months   =
The above information was last updated on   22.10.89

continued..........

CCN 185

- 4 -

CAIS Account Details (Continued)

Miss A Anybody, Sure Finance, Defaulted Account,
Amount of Debt at 06/89, £88

Current Status   9
Status History
Total Status 2 in last   months   =
Total Status 3 in last   months   =
The above information was last updated on   30.07.89

Current Status
Status History
Total Status 2 in last   months   =
Total Status 3 in last   months   =
The above information was last updated on

Current Status
Status History
Total Status 2 in last   months   =
Total Status 3 in last   months   =
The above information was last updated on

Current Status
Status History
Total Status 2 in last   months   =
Total Status 3 in last   months   =
The above information was last updated on

Current Status
Status History
Total Status 2 in last   months   =
Total Status 3 in last   months   =
The above information was last updated on

CCN Systems

continued..........

CCN 186

EXPLANATION OF TERMS USED

The use of the term 'since...' when confirming names on the electoral register does not imply that the persons listed have only been registered since that date, but rather that CCN Systems Limited has only been able to confirm the family at the address since that year.

The number '18' after an elector's name indicates that that person was recorded as reaching that age on the most recent electoral register to be processed by CCN Systems Limited.

Where account information is shown, the balance is that provided to CCN Systems Limited at the last update. Any payment made between that date and the date the file is supplied will not be shown but will be included at the next update.

With the exception of electoral roll information, all the dates are shown on the file as a month followed by a year. For example, 01/84 is the first month in 1984 (January 1984).

Judgment information includes the source of that information.

Source	Meaning
LCH	County Court Judgment obtained from the Lord Chancellors Dept
SGSC	Scottish Decree obtained from Stubb's Gazette. Scottish Edition
SGEI	Judgment obtained from Stubb's Gazette, Republic of Ireland
SGNI	Judgment obtained from Stubb's Gazette, Northern Ireland Edition

County Court Judgments have details of the court and plaint note number provided where possible. Any judgment which has been paid and for which a Certificate of Satisfaction has been obtained will be shown by a date and the word 'Satisfied'.

- 5 -

ADDRESS SEARCHES

The following lists dates and names of Companies who have searched CCN Systems records at the addresses shown on this form. Please note, a search made against an address is not necessarily a credit search, nor indeed a search made in respect of the subject of this enquiry.

Present Address

18.11.89 Tipco Credit
17.10.89 Mishmash Clothing
30.09.89 Noworth

Appendix IV.3

XYZ LIMITED SCORECARD: PART 1

Years in present employment	0-5 0	6-10 15	11-12 30	Over 12 50	
Marital status	Divorced 0	Widowed 10	Married 40	Single 12	
Time at current residence	Less than 6 mths 5	6 mths - 4 yrs 7	5-8 yrs 12	Over 8 yrs 22	
Time with bank	< 3 mths 0	3 mths - 1 yr 0	1 yr 1 mth - 3 yrs 30	> 3 yrs 1 mth 30	No account 25
Age of most recent bad debt	No debts 5	Under 3 mths −35	4-12 mths −30	1-2 yrs −27	2-3 yrs -15
Age	21-25 0	26-30 5	31-39 40	40-59 55	60 + 42

XYZ LIMITED SCORECARD: PART 2

Telephone	Yes +20	No −30	Not Answered 0		
Source of application	A −10	B 0	C 10	D 20	
Region	1 −25	2 0	3 10	4 20	5 30
Accommodation status	Owner 30	Tenant 0	living with parent 10	Other −10	
No. of children	None 30	1 15	2 5	+3 0	
Occupation	A −10	B 0	C 10	D 20	

Appendix IV.4
Data protection aspects of credit referencing: what happens
in Denmark, France, West Germany, Norway and Sweden

Denmark

In Denmark, credit information is covered in part 3 of the *Private Registers Act 1978*. Credit information bureaux are one of the categories of data holders required with the *Registertilsynet*, or *Data Surveillance Authority (DSA)*, which also has direct control over them. In 1988 16 bureaux had registered with the DSA. There were also 71 agencies operating blacklists - designed to warn other organisations about bad credit or other risks. These companies must receive permission from the Authority *in advance* of setting up.

In 1988 the DSA reported that they had received 568 formal queries about data use in the private sector. A quarter of these were complaints. Of these, 29 per cent were on credit information; the DSA considered the complaints to be justified in nearly three-quarters of cases.

1. THE INFORMATION

Credit reference bureaux may only store and transfer information which is less than 5 years old (except where it is of "overriding importance" for assessing the creditworthiness of the data subject). It must be relevant for assessing the data subject's creditworthiness.

2. ACCESS

Data subjects on whom details are kept, apart from their names and addresses, must be informed that a record is kept, at most four weeks after the information is deposited. The information sent to them must inform them of their rights of access to the records on them.

If a data subject wishes to see his file, the company must inform him of all the data it has, including any information and assessments it has passed to a third party within the last six months. S/he must also be told of the right to inspect the data.

Credit information, in summary form, can only be released to third parties who are subscribers to the bureaux. Information such as PIN numbers may not be released.

3. RECENT CHANGES TO THE LAW

Two amendments were made to Denmark's Private Registers Act in April 1988.

Summary information can be released only on the basis of a *named individual*. In effect this means that using information based on address (which would include other third party information) is deemed to be irrelevant, and is no longer permitted.

Credit information companies may release data on debts only when the information has a published source (the *Danish Official Gazette*) or is for debts over DKr.1,000 (about £80.00) to one creditor (in the latter case the debtor must have given the creditor written agreement that the debt is due); or additionally, if the debt is the subject of court action for recovery. However, the presence of a court order for repayment can only be passed on if the obligation is still outstanding. If the individual has been released from the obligation, he is no longer considered to be a debtor, and so the information on the court order cannot be released.

4. CORRECTION OF MISLEADING DATA

These rights are similar to those enjoyed in the UK under our own Data Protection Act. However, once a correction or amendment has been filed and a copy sent to the data subject, this must also be sent to all third parties receiving a copy of the file in the previous six months. The data subject must also be told of any third party which has been sent the written correction.

5. ACCESS FEES

The Danish Ministry of Justice has set an access fee of a maximum DKr10 (80p) for a short summary or DKr50 (£4) per page for longer reports.

6. COURT ACTIONS

Up to April 1989 there had only been one court case involving credit information. A credit information company refused to give information to a data subject on its source of incorrect information. The company was fined on a daily basis until it agreed to release the source of the data.

France

The *Data Processing, Data Files and Individual Liberties Act* came into force in January 1978, after eight years of investigation and drafting. It also established an independent authority - *Commission Nationale de l'Informatique et des Libertés (CNIL)* to regulate, monitor and oversee data protection.

In general, when collecting data, the people supplying the information must be informed of the following:

★ whether supplying the information is voluntary or mandatory, and the consequences if they do not do so;

★ who will hold the data;

★ the period for which the data will be held;

★ their rights of access and correction.

1. CREDIT INFORMATION

CNIL has been examining the problems of consumer credit information (considered to be a sensitive subject), regularly since 1980. Working with the industry it adopted a simplified and standard practice in 1980. This was subsequently modified both in 1985 and more recently in July 1988, partly due to the increased use of automated credit scoring, and to reduce the number of complaints to the CNIL about refusals to grant credit.

2. CREDIT SCORING

CNIL considers that the increased use of automated credit scoring in risk assessment has a specific impact on individual vulnerability. Scoring requires the assessment of characteristics such as age, marital status, years in a particular home, and number of years in a job. These are compared against data drawn from similar, composite profiles of known good and bad credit risks. CNIL therefore considers that the decision to lend may be made on an individual without any guarantee that his/her individual characteristics are respected.

In 1988, CNIL revised its recommendation on the use of credit information, to include more safeguards (see below).

3. CREDIT INFORMATION RECOMMENDATION

Any decision to grant or refuse credit must not be based solely on "the automated processing of data defining the profile or the personality of the person requesting the loan" (i.e. credit scoring alone).

If refused credit as a result of credit scoring, the individual has a right to know, and contest the information. This right extends to the reasoning used for automatic data processing. (In effect, being told the *logic* behind the automated credit scoring.)

Those seeking a loan must be told that if they fall behind with their payments, the information will be put into a "bad payers" file, and made available to the credit industry.

"Bad payers" are considered to be those borrowers who reach a serious level of default - for example, those who fail to make three repayments. This is the norm of the Banking Commission.

If a person is refused credit as a result of information from a reference agency's bad payers file, the company must tell the applicant this, and the source of the information.

Those whose names are put into a bad payers file must be informed beforehand, or when this step is taken.

All possible precautions must be taken to avoid confusing people with the same name; surname should be accompanied by first name, date and place of birth, and other identifying characteristics.

Rights of access are similar to the UK legislation.

Federal Republic of Germany

The *Federal Data Protection Act* was adopted in 1977 and came fully into force in 1979. In Germany, much of the enforcement responsibility devolves to the Lander (state) authorities.

Consumer credit aspects of data protection are regulated by principles within the Data Protection Act and not by specific sections in it (as in Norway) nor by a separate Act (as in Sweden). Credit reference agencies are directly supervised by the eleven Lander data protection authorities.

1. CREDIT INFORMATION COMPANIES

Credit information companies are allowed to store personal data, provided there is no reason to assume that the interests of the data subject will be harmed. They must inform the individual that they are storing information on them. This means the data subject can then exercise his/her right of access to check the accuracy of the record. A fee is charged that must "not exceed the costs directly attributable to the provision of information". Generally companies do not charge an access fee, but credit reference agencies typically charged Dm.10-15 (about £3.10-£4.70).

They are allowed to pass on personal data to those seeking credit information on individuals. Only those lenders contributing information are given access to the database.

The major credit reference agency is the *SCHUFA (Protective Association for General Credit Precautions)* which was founded in 1927. It comprises about 13 independent organisations operating at a state level, but co-operating under the SCHUFA rulebook. There is a data bank on about 21 million people, and stores of information about individuals' loans. The agencies store both positive and negative information.

Positive information: Disclosing this information to the agency requires the express consent of the individual, who at the same time is told where the information will be held, and what it will be used for. However, as in the United States, a refusal is generally likely to result in withdrawal of the offer of credit. The information includes details of existence of a credit agreement, the credit limit, and methods of repayment. It will record whether the repayment schedule has been met. It contains bank credit (but not other account) details, mail order company and retail credit transactions. While the information is predominantly on unsecured loans, some information on mortgages is now being lodged (mainly at the discretion of the banks, and with the appropriate express consent).

Negative information: Storing this information may be done without the express consent of the individual. It includes details of summonses (if not disputed by the borrower), and judgement debts; default of two months or more (after the borrower has been informed in writing that such negative data is being registered); also, if credit card facilities have been withdrawn, this will be shown. If overdrafts have not been agreed with the bank, these details may also be stored. Information may be held on file for five years, although it is generally kept for only three years.

Agencies and lenders also have recourse to other public registers on debt, bankruptcy and, provided they can prove a legitimate interest, details of large outstanding mortgages on properties.

Third party information: Taking account of third party information in credit risk assessment, as used in the UK, is not permitted in the Federal Republic. However, when a legal relationship exists - such as a joint credit agreement between husband and wife, or the payment of maintenance to a former spouse, such information may be supplied to the lender. Making sure of an individual's identity is, of course, greatly helped by the use of identity cards; also lenders are required to maintain high standards of accuracy in surname, full forenames and address. Information on date and place of birth may also be collected (with the individual's consent), and if necessary used as another positive identifier.

Norway

The *Personal Data Registers Act* was adopted in 1978 and came into force in January 1980. Amendments, covering enforcement and the use of credit information, were passed in 1987, shortly followed by further amendments on direct marketing and telephone marketing.

Credit information is covered by Chapter 5 of the Act, and is enforced by the *Data Inspectorate (DI)*. A company must get prior permission to start a credit information agency, and in 1988 the DI licensed 13 companies to operate such services. They are only allowed to provide credit information - undertaking any other "personal information service" is prohibited.

Apart from independent credit information companies, there is also a government-owned public register - the *Losoreregisterit* in northern Norway at Bronnoysund. This register is also licensed by the DI, which monitors the quality of the data.

1. THE INFORMATION

The government register keeps information on housing and related mortgages, cars and related loans; company business loans; property agreements between spouses, and data on bad payers/bad debts.

Data are generally held for three years, although exceptionally "information of substantial significance for a proper assessment" may be held for more than three years.

2. CONSUMER REDRESS

One of the main principles underlying the Act is that a credit information company must take responsibility for the quality of the data. Even if it comes from a normally accurate source, the company is still liable for damages if information is incorrect, erroneous or misleading.

3. DISCLOSURE

Interestingly, part of the Act states that credit information must not be disclosed if the person requesting it has insufficient justification for gaining access to it. It could be expected that endless arguments occur over whether an application was "justified" or not. But in practice there has been only one complaint to the DI on this point. This is largely a result of the requirement in s.20, which ensures that everyone on whom information is *requested* is sent a copy of their record; at the same time they must be told the identity of the person who has requested the information. The data subject does not pay a fee for this service.

4. ACCESS

Individuals and companies have a right to be informed in writing of the information a company has on them for credit assessment use. They will also be told the information on them that has been released in the previous six months; who requested it, and from whom the credit company has received information.

Companies may charge a "reasonable" fee for this - informally set at around NKr.50-100 (about £4-£8). This is the *only* point in the data protection law where an organisation may charge an access fee - because it is one way for data subjects (who may not be applying for credit at the time) to check their creditworthiness.

5. THIRD PARTY INFORMATION

The main limitations on the use of third party data in assessing an individual's creditworthiness are the principles ensuring that the information should not be used for forming "an unjustified or unreasonably negative judgement" regarding a person (s.15 of the Act).

In addition, credit reference companies may not use information concerning family affairs other than "that referring to family relationships or family status, property arrangements between spouses and bread-winner status" (s.16.5).

Like other European and Scandinavian countries, Norway operates a national registration system, with all citizens having an identity number.

6. INFORMED CONSENT

There are no specific rules on the way in which consumers give their informed consent for the disclosure of information which may form part of a credit profile. Credit information agencies cannot force individuals or companies to answer questions. Banks, finance houses and other potential lenders are free to make the loan or not, or to vary the interest rate they charge. Up to 1988 the DI had not received any complaints on this point.

Sweden

Sweden has the distinction of passing the world's first data protection law, in 1973. But this was long preceded by the *Freedom of the Press Act*, passed in 1766, which gives the public access to government information in general, and its counterpart the *Secrecy Act*, which lists exemptions. These include the protection of individual privacy regarding medical and financial information.

The *1973 Data Act*, plus the *Credit Information Act 1973* and *Debt Recovery Act 1974*, regulate privacy in the financial and credit area. Credit information is considered to be "sensitive data" and holders must be registered and licensed by the *Data Inspection Board (DIB)*. Licences expire after ten years and businesses have to re-apply.

The DIB also handles complaints and imposes sanctions. There were 783 complaints in the first ten years of the Act, but this has been steadily increasing. In 1987/88 there were 552 complaints, the largest categories of which related to debt collecting and consumer credit information.

THE CREDIT INFORMATION ACT 1973 (amended 1981, 1982, 1984 and 1988)
1. THE INFORMATION

Credit information companies may store or transfer only negative credit information. This includes default on repayments that have reached the court stage, court judgements, bankruptcies, or otherwise failing to keep to a settlement agreed with creditors. The DIB has the discretion to add further categories of data, and has done so recently in order to let credit card companies register information on misuse of credit cards.

An individual's credit record must be cleaned of information more than three years old.

2. DISCLOSURE

Personal information may be supplied only to a party who needs it for concluding a credit agreement with the data subject, or for a "similar reason". This may include checking the creditworthiness of a prospective tenant.

When credit information on an individual is supplied for credit reference purposes, a written copy must be provided free of charge to the data subject. This must include the contents of the file, the assessment of credit risk, advice given to the prospective lender, and the identity of the individual or organisation which has requested the information.

Data subjects have the right to be informed of whether a credit information company has a record on them and, if so, to obtain a copy. The company may charge a "reasonable fee" which the DIB currently interprets as SKr.50 (just over £4.00) for an average record of one to one and a half pages and pro rata for longer records.

3. INFORMED CONSENT

Data subjects do *not* have a right of prior consent or veto over the release of a record on themselves that may form part of a consumer creditworthiness profile. However, data subjects have a right under s.11 of the Act to be informed "at the same time" that information on them has been released. They will also receive a copy of the contents of the file.

4. THIRD PARTY INFORMATION

Using third party information in credit risk assessment is prohibited. Section 5 of the Act states that credit information activities must be conducted in such a way that they do not result in encroachment on personal privacy. This may be through the content of the information supplied, or in any other way, or in the storage or delivery of incorrect or misleading information.

5. CONSUMER REDRESS

An individual has the right to claim compensation for material or immaterial damages if his/her privacy has been violated, or incorrect information has been released.

Index

Printed in the United Kingdom for HMSO
Dd240095 4/90 C35 G443 10170